What They're Saying about *The Organized M...*

"If you are looking for clarity and peac[...] [...]tacey Crew shows you that getting ready f[...] [...]ming, but can be fun and exciting. So get rea[...]

Kimberley Clayton Blaine, MA, MFT; f[...] and author, *Mommy Confidence: 8 Easy Steps to Reclaiming Balance, Motivation and Your Inner Diva*

"As a pediatrician who is dedicated to simplifying the lives of new moms, this book is number one on my list. *The Organized Mom* provides moms-to-be with a blue-print not just for organizing the nursery, but for organizing their new lives. Stacey Crew keeps the focus on what is most important—creating uncluttered spaces to live in, and opening up time to enjoy being a new parent."

Mary Ann LoFrumento, MD, pediatrician and author of *Simply Parenting: Understanding Your Newborn & Infant*

"*The Organized Mom* is the perfect guide for a busy first-time mother like me. It breaks down the concept into easy-to-understand, manageable tasks that will change your way of thinking and make for a much smoother lifestyle. Less time on laundry and cleaning—more time with my family!!!"

Terry Haas, a featured real estate agent on HGTV's hit show *Designed to Sell*

"Great read for any new mom looking to organize and prepare herself, home, and nursery for the little one on the way! *The Organized Mom* outlines 'real mommy' tips and techniques that include the list of must-haves for each room in the house, what you need and how to organize the nursery, and what to pack in the hospital suitcase. Our customers look to us to 'make it easy.' As a professional organizer and mom herself, Crew walks you through the steps to do just that. Being orga-nized reduces stress and gives you more time to enjoy your family and new baby."

Deborah Shearer, co-owner of Organize.com

"Everything you need to know, including answers to questions you might never have thought to ask! Whether you're expecting your first or your fifth baby, you'll be glad you read this book."

Donna Smallin, author of *The One-Minute Organizer A to Z Storage Solutions*, www.unclutter.com

What They're Saying about *The Organized Mom*

"Take it from an organizationally impaired mother of four, Stacey Crew's GOPACK method is a lifeline! *The Organized Mom* offers comprehensive chaos control, room by room, so that women can have everything in place to enjoy the amazing gift of a new baby."

> Emily Abedon, contributor to *American Baby, Parents, Child, Lamaze Family, Redbook*, and Grandparents.com

"An organizing essential! Clear and concise, Stacey Crew doesn't only make the task of organizing the home for baby less daunting, she makes it sound fun. The strategies in this book will give new parents the ability to spend less time organizing and cleaning, and more time enjoying parenthood."

> Bridgette Raes, Bridgette Raes Style Group, *www.bridgetteraes.com*, author of *Style Rx: Dressing the Body You Have to Create the Body You Want*

"Stacey Crew is every new mom's personal assistant. She guides new moms through what they need and how to use it to make their lives easier. *The Organized Mom* is a commonsense approach to guarantee stress-free days in the chaotic world of motherhood."

> Mary Jo Rulnick, author of *The Frantic Woman's Guide* Series

"As a work-at-home mom with a young child, I always need good ideas for making my house and my life more organized. *The Organized Mom* provides plenty of practical advice for how to organize before your baby arrives as well as useful tips for those of us who already have children."

> Holly Fisher, freelance writer/editor, the Green Office Blog (greenofficeprojects.org/blog)

"What a great, easy-to-read resource. You don't even need to be an expecting mom to benefit from this book, with so many great ideas for organizing your home and life. Thanks, Stacey!"

> Adam Levy, cofounder, Zwaggle.com

Dear New Mom,

When I started to think about writing a book about organizing for new moms I was a relatively new mom myself. When I started writing this book, my daughters were two and almost five. And now, my little one just turned nine and my oldest is in sixth grade. What I know for sure is that time passes quickly and the more organized you are, the more you are able to enjoy the precious and fleeting time you have with your baby. In many ways, I feel like I blinked and the time was gone.

Now, as a mom who has written two books, who contributes regularly to local and national publications and websites, and who has a full-time organizing and consulting business, I have many happy memories of baby time. Being organized can make all the difference between being a constantly frazzled new mom and a more relaxed, much *less* frazzled new mom.

I remember what it was like to be overwhelmed with baby gear and baby needs and family demands. In fact, I don't think there is another time in women's lives when we are bombarded with more information than it feels humanly possible to handle. Plus, we're taking care of that precious and helpless little human who is completely relying on us for his or her every need!

So why do you need this book? Because it is filled with simple, smart ideas you can apply right now so that you can begin to feel in charge and competent. These ideas will help you figure out what baby gear you really need and how to put it in a logical place in your home. So much of parenthood is dealing with the *unexpected* events in any given day—this book will help you manage everything else.

Treat this book as a trusted friend—turn to it for both specific advice and big-picture planning so that these wonderful moments don't pass you by. Enjoy the ride and don't forget to make time for you.

Stacey Crew

the
organized
mom

**SIMPLIFY LIFE FOR
YOU AND BABY,
ONE STEP AT A TIME**

Stacey Crew, founder of the GOPACK® Method

adamsmedia
Avon, Massachusetts

Published by
Adams Media, a division of F+W Media, Inc.
57 Littlefield Street, Avon, MA 02322. U.S.A.
www.adamsmedia.com

ISBN 10: 1-60550-130-1
ISBN 13: 978-1-60550-130-7

Printed in China.

J I H G F E D C B A

Library of Congress Cataloging-in-Publication Data
is available from the publisher.

This publication is designed to provide accurate and authoritative information
with regard to the subject matter covered. It is sold with the understanding
that the publisher is not engaged in rendering legal, accounting, or other
professional advice. If legal advice or other expert assistance is required, the
services of a competent professional person should be sought.
—From a *Declaration of Principles* jointly adopted by a Committee of the
American Bar Association and a Committee of Publishers and Associations

Many of the designations used by manufacturers and sellers to distinguish
their product are claimed as trademarks. Where those designations appear in
this book and Adams Media was aware of a trademark claim, the designations have been printed with initial capital letters.

The GOPACK® system is a registered trademark of Stacey Crew.

Names of women in "Problem—Solved!" sections were changed to protect
the identity of clients.

Interior illustrations by Eric Andrews.

This book is available at quantity discounts for bulk purchases.
For information, please call 1-800-289-0963.

Contents

Acknowledgments

The writing process is different for everyone, but I think most writers would tell you that the last efforts to complete a manuscript feel monumental at times. With that in mind, there are quite a few people I need to thank for their support during the process of completing this book:

My daughters, Claire and Jenna, who are my daily inspiration and keep me grounded and hopeful in a world filled with negativity. They are my shining beacons and the reasons that I'm a better person today! My mom, Cathy Brady, whose pep talks, encouraging words, and faith in me over the years kept me going and gets me back on track when I'm feeling worn out. My sister, Carolyn Murphy, helped me to understand what true commitment means and the importance of persevering when you feel extremely passionate about something.

My girlfriends! My mom's advice was right when I would complain of heartbreak as a teenager: "You'll always have your girlfriends so cherish those relationships," she would tell me. And she was right. Good girlfriends are worth the time to find and keep. You know who you are—thank you!

To the experts in their fields who provided input for the book: Kathleen Schulweis, PhD, my coach and mentor, who knows how to dig deep and get to the heart of the matter while maintaining grace and integrity in her profession. Melissa Leonard for her enthusiasm, optimism, and the wonderful teachings she brings us through her expertise in the field of etiquette. Bridgette Raes, stylist and author of *Style Rx*, is an amazing example of a woman who goes after her dream and makes it a reality. She was the impetus for my trip to New York City in search of an agent and publisher. Dr. Lauren Hamilton, who delivered both my babies, and who I respect enormously for her dedication to her profession and her ability to ask the difficult questions . . . and her willingness to listen to the answers. Dr. Mary Ann LoFrumento, who encouraged my simple philosophy and shares the same in her own book, *Understanding Your Newborn & Infant*. Lara Allison, DVM, for her expertise on introducing your new baby to your pet. Karen Leach, Los Angeles photographer, who takes amazing photos of babies. And, of course, my Literary Crew: My agent, Barbara Poelle, whose wit, humor, and professionalism helped me achieve one of my biggest dreams and maintain my focus and, at times, enthusiasm during challenging times throughout this process. Chelsea King at Adams Media, who believed in the project and brought the book to life. My editor, Laura Daly, who is a new mom herself and a fantastic editor, took the book to new heights through her skillful editing. From the depths of my heart, thank you to all three of you!

Finally, thanks to all the moms who I met during the process of writing this book. The young woman with the three-week-old baby with whom I spoke briefly at Barnes & Noble one morning, my wonderful mom clients who have undertaken the enormity of raising children and are doing it well, and the women about to have their first babies—thank you!

Introduction

Congratulations! Pregnancy is such a special time. It's a time for wondering, dreaming, and even some introspection. You're likely thinking about your baby whenever you have a free moment. Who will this baby look like? What kind of personality will she have? Will he have Uncle Jack's ears? What about my darling husband's eyes and deep sensitivity?

And it is certainly a time when you need to plan, plan, and plan. How will you set up a space in your home for your new little person? What do you really need and where will you put it all? *The Organized Mom* will help you determine exactly what you need and where to put it, using my proven, step-by-step GOPACK method for getting and staying organized. The book is designed to guide you—the mom-to-be—through the preparation of the nursery, packing for the hospital stay, and staying organized once baby arrives. *The Organized Mom* also contains helpful information about baby's first year, including how to: analyze your childcare options, successfully transition from a couple to a family, and plan a perfect first birthday party. At the back of the book, you will find resources on everything from baby announcements to child safety to storage solutions to product recalls.

What Is Organizing, Anyway?

Organizing is: Having respect for your belongings. If you have too much of something, you don't necessarily appreciate it as much as if you had only one cherished item. And what about the items you can't even locate because they're at the bottom of a jam-packed closet or in a drawer covered with other items that are not being used?

Organizing is: Being prepared for what life throws your way. Being prepared for baby's arrival will help you ease into motherhood in a more relaxed state. *The Organized Mom* will help you organize the details so

part one

organizing

your home

01 | Transitional Organizing: What Is It?

Major life changes and transitions are generally what throw people into the greatest state of disorganization. Think about these common scenarios:

- **A job change:** Changing jobs requires physical and mental dedication, and can lead to a new schedule or not having the amount of time to address routine household maintenance issues.
- **A move:** If you've moved from a larger place to a smaller place, you may lack storage. Or if you've moved into a larger house, you may be in the process of accumulating furniture and accessories.
- **Getting married or moving in with your partner:** Combining two households can be overwhelming because you are attempting to merge items that potentially come from different styles and tastes. It's all a natural process that is very exciting, but it can also be overwhelming because you are settling into a new way of life and possibly new surroundings.

These are generally not times of decluttering, but instead are about combining and accumulating stuff. Motherhood is one of these times when we are inundated with all sorts of gear—bottles, diapers, toys, and tiny pieces of clothing. All those items can leave new moms wondering where to put them and how to maintain some sort of organized systems once baby arrives. The key buzzwords today are *decluttering* and *organizing*. However, when you're a new mom, to a certain extent, it's all about cluttering—like the scenarios we just talked about. It's challenging to stay on top of everything when you're caring for a new baby *and* accumulating and managing all of his or her gear! That is why many new moms experience a slew of emotions that can potentially contribute to postpartum depression and feelings of disappointment because what is supposed to be a most blissful time has turned out to be stressful.

Preparing and organizing before a new baby arrives can certainly help ease the potential anxiety and help simplify your surroundings so you get to spend quality time with your bundle of joy!

What's It Worth?

When it comes to organizing, the goal is to know what you have and where it is. And there's more to it than just having a place for everything. In today's economy, it's important to give thought to how much space you're giving to a particular category/item. Most people take a passive stance on managing their belongings. They look at what they have and put it somewhere, rather than deciding how much space to allow for a specific category/function, then fitting the appropriate amount of stuff into that space. Setting space limits may require downsizing what you have in a particular category—for example, collectibles, arts and crafts materials, gardening equipment, clothing, kitchen items, and so on.

Determining how much space you will give to a particular item/category and where those items will live gives you more control over your stuff. No matter where you live, you only have a finite amount of space. Unless you're planning to move to a larger home, it's important to assess the existing space and how it's being used to ensure you're getting the most from your real estate investment. Think of it in terms of your *financial* investment (whether you rent or own).

Owning

Do the math and figure out how much your home's square footage is worth (dividing the amount you purchased your home for by its square footage). For a home, the value might be something like $125 per square foot, or as high as $250 to $500 if you live in California or a major city. To figure out the value of a specific space, simply take its measurements. If you have a 10' × 10' room, that's 100 square feet. Therefore, the value of the space in that room, based on $125 per square foot, is $12,500. If the room is completely cluttered, $12,500 of your overall real estate investment may be unusable. Look at the closets. The average size of a master bedroom walk-in closet is 6' × 8', or a total of 48 square feet. At $125 per square foot, that closet is worth $6,000. Do you currently have a closet jammed full of unused, unrecognizable items? You know, the closet that you're afraid to go into?

The point being, many people invest in McMansions, thinking that they really need the extra space. In reality, many of them could actually live in smaller spaces if they were more considerate about the value of their things and how much space they want to give to those items.

Renting

Determining your real estate investment can also be equated to a rental situation. If your rent is $1,200 per month for a 900-square-foot apartment, you're paying $1.33 per square foot or $133.00 per month for a 10' × 10' room. If you have that room devoted to storage, ask yourself whether you'd be better off renting a storage facility for perhaps $50/month or reclaiming the space altogether by decluttering and making it a functional space. Couples often wonder how they'll make space for baby in a small city apartment, when the spare room is currently being used as an office or storage area. So consider the money you're paying for the space and make some decisions.

 good idea!
If you're considering moving or relocating, visit Salary.com's cost-of-living calculator to see what you get for your money.

Put Yourself in the Driver's Seat

So when you're organizing your crafts or your collectibles, ask yourself, "How much real estate do I want to give these items?" And instead of taking a passive role in this line of questioning and saying to yourself, "I don't have enough room for all this stuff," try reframing the language and instead say, "I'm going to allow half of my guest room closet to hold my craft supplies. Since I'm only allowing my crafts to take up this much space, I need to make a decision. I either take space from another category or I pare down what I currently have to fit that real estate."

Changing your perspective and the language you use will help you get the results you seek because you are empowered—you are no longer ruled by what you own. You become the ruler and have the last word.

Organizing Versus Cleaning: There *Is* a Difference

As an organizing expert, it's important for me to make the distinction between cleaning and organizing because many people attempt to lump these two functions together. Although some of you may perform these functions simultaneously, they are distinct. In my experience, both personally and with my clients, cleaning is a lot easier and faster when things are decluttered and organized. You can cut your cleaning time dramatically if all items have a home. The reason: You don't have to move all the clutter to clean off countertops, shelving units, floors, tables, and so on.

Let me define both terms:

Cleaning: Dusting and vacuuming. It's the act of making something clean; removing stains or spots.
Organizing: Arranging and putting items into an orderly, functional whole.

Organizing is the critical step in preparing your house for regular cleaning. I can't tell you how many times I've heard people say that they needed to "straighten up" for the housekeeper, which essentially means "organizing" for the housekeeper. How many times is that left until the last minute, so the stuff you're "organizing" simply gets tossed into a closet or drawers so that the countertops can be cleaned off? Meanwhile, there's a mess behind those closed doors and drawers.

Organizing is the process of eliminating the excess and finding a place for everything so that when it comes time to straighten up, you simply have to put the items where they belong . . . and putting the mail on the kitchen counter or the pile of newspapers on the front hall table is not going to make it easy for you to clean up.

At this point, I'd like to dispel the notion that you can get organized on a Saturday morning, despite what you might have read or heard elsewhere. You could organize one specific area in that amount of time, but not an entire home. Organizing is truly a process, and to achieve long-lasting results with any process it's necessary to first assess the situation, and next to formulate a plan.

How to Be an Organized Mom

As a new mom, you're seeking direction and advice. That's part of the reason you're reading this book—to collect information to effectively organize your time and space. Well, I want to help you understand that no matter what information you collect, it's important that you listen to that inner voice—or gut instinct—before making any final decisions. Here are other things to consider while you're amassing new knowledge.

Make Conscious Decisions

First, and most important, you should begin thinking consciously about your intentions. As you make the shift from couple to family, you will need to make many choices and decisions. Take shopping, for example. You will be inundated with opportunities to spend money to make the "perfect" space for your baby, and you will find that family and friends alike will have all sorts of opinions about what you must have, should have, and can do without.

It's easy to be influenced by other's opinions and suggestions, especially if that person has already been through the experience. However, we all have different perspectives. What works for one person may not work for you. Politely listen and consider the suggestions, but always do what you think is right for you.

If you take time to tap into your instincts, the next time you're presented with a choice or decision, you'll know to slow down and let your gut tell you what's right. Collect as much information as possible, but remember—there's a lot of information out there that will not be suited to you, your values, or your lifestyle, as well as information that will conflict with your core beliefs, such as if you have a strong belief in breastfeeding versus bottle feeding. You will need to treat each piece of information like you would a dish on a buffet: Take what you like best and leave the rest. It can be as simple as that.

Problem — Solved!

When Sandra was pregnant, she had many people around her telling her she needed to buy this, attend that class, eat this, and wear that. Initially, she took many of the suggestions, but she quickly became tired and confused. It wasn't long before she began to realize that *everyone* had an opinion. While Sandra sorted through much of this unsolicited advice, a good friend matter-of-factly said, "You know what's best for you, Sandra. Use the same instincts you use in business. You've always done well that way."

Sandra began to slow down a bit and tap into her inner voice. The answers started to come with little frustration.

Take the Time to Plan

Planning is an essential step in the process of organizing. Have you ever said to yourself, "On Saturday I'm going to get organized." Then Saturday comes, and you achieve very little. That's because there was no forethought or plan. Without a plan, you don't have a course of action to follow to achieve your goal; it's also impossible to discern whether you achieved the results you wanted. That said, it's hard to plan if you don't know what you need, as is often the case with having a new baby. That's where *The Organized Mom* and the GOPACK method come in.

Problem — Solved!

The GOPACK method helped Liz and Mike sort out their space problem. They lived in a two-bedroom and used one of the bedrooms as a home office for Mike's business. They thought that they would need to relocate his office outside the home to use the space for the nursery. Although Mike felt he could be more productive having his office at home because he could periodically help care for the baby, Liz felt that the baby needed her own room where they could zone a sleeping area, changing/dressing area, and a play area. After talking further, they also realized that Mike could more easily focus on business at hand if he didn't have the distractions of baby. The compromise: Mike would work most of the day at an office outside the home, but be available to work from home if Liz needed to run errands without baby in tow. The couple carved out a work space for Mike in the family room area that was strictly for his laptop and portable file box. When Mike wasn't using the desk, Liz could use it to send notes or pay bills. Planning in advance helped Liz and Mike create a nursery, make space for particular activities, and minimize clutter in their small space.

Get Some Support

Everyone needs support, especially a new mom. You need encouragement, feedback, and validation. Support manifests itself in many different forms: family, friends, moms' groups, and caregivers (inside and outside the home). Whether you stay at home or return to work you will want to enlist help in one form or another. Raising children truly does require help. Whether it comes from family, friends, childcare service, or other new moms—*get it* and *take it* when someone offers!

Problem—Solved!

Maryann is a professional woman who quickly discovered that in spite of having a master's degree in education and running a successful consulting business for many years, she was at her wits' end when her baby boy was about four weeks old. The lack of sleep and the unplanned lack of support from her husband (who just two days after the baby's birth was back on military duty and unavailable) was taking its toll.

Most of Maryann's friends were either single or married without children; she was the first in her group to take the leap into motherhood. As a result, she felt alone and unsupported, through no fault of her friends—they just hadn't been there or done that yet. And Maryann's family lived out of state.

Fortunately, Maryann had a neighbor who looked in on her and could see that she was exhausted and didn't know what to do about it. The neighbor gave her the telephone number of a nearby woman who had two children and was active in meeting other moms. Reluctantly, Maryann called Emily, who invited Maryann over for lunch the next day.

Emily recognized the stress Maryann was under and helped Maryann open up and share what was happening. Emily told Maryann that she was miserable. One minute she was terribly resentful and overwhelmed with feelings of guilt, and then the next she would look into the baby's eyes and feel overwhelmed with love. It was the universal oxymoron that most moms experience from time to time.

From that time on, Maryann began to connect with other women. The support helped her deal with the daily challenges that come with being a mom. Her guilt began to subside and she was more easily able to identify those moments when she felt helpless and do something about it before she fell into a slump.

Be Aware of How Much You Own

Most of us are inundated with stuff and buy bigger homes to accommodate it all rather than evaluating what we have and why we need it.

The "P," or Purge, aspect of the GOPACK method introduces the process of deciding what to keep, what to get rid of, and where to store what you keep (see Chapter 3 for the complete step-by-step method).

Problem — Solved!

Selena wanted to create a dream nursery for her new baby. However, the room she wanted to use was packed with stuff—a treadmill that was covered with Christmas decorations, a dresser that was overflowing with old papers, a bookcase that had an unused printer on it, and a closet filled with boxes that contained belongings she had been given after her grandmother passed away. "Where do I begin?" was Selena's big question.

The GOPACK method helped Selena decide how to organize what was in the room that would become the nursery. First, she grouped objects together—all of the Christmas decorations that had not been moved to the attic, for example. She tossed some old artificial garland, placed the remaining decorations in containers, labeled them, and stored them in the attic. She then followed the same approach with the other items in the room.

Once the treadmill was moved to the garage and the room was essentially clear, Selena used the steps outlined in Chapter 4, Organizing the Nursery, to make the space baby-friendly.

Value Your Time

According to a study published by Salary.com in May 2008, moms work an average of 94.4 hours per week (both "working" and stay-at-home moms). Their value translated into salary is $117,000 annually for stay-at-home moms. For working moms (40 hours per week), there's an excess of 54.6 hours per week, which translates into an additional

$68,405 annually. So when you purchase something for $50, how many hours did you have to work to pay for it?

As a new mom, you'll need to carefully choose how you spend your time, and if you attach a dollar value to it you may be more likely to choose family time over volunteering your time elsewhere, as well as creating ways to become more efficient. For example, organizing and putting systems in place will help you to become more efficient.

Problem—Solved!

Caroline and Phillip knew that once their baby arrived, they'd be pressed for time alone. They also knew that finding time to pursue their separate personal activities would be a challenge. Together, they established some personal, couple, and family goals in an attempt to maintain some of their existing activities and couple time as well as quality family time with the new baby.

To accomplish the goals, Caroline quickly realized she would need to make a few adjustments. She signed up with a reputable sitter service so she and Phillip could go out from time to time. Currently, spare time wasn't an issue; however, she knew when baby arrived it would become increasingly challenging to go out with her girlfriends on a regular basis. She spoke with Phillip and they each agreed that they would give each other at least one night a month to separately go out with friends. Phillip realized that if he wanted to continue running five days a week that it may be necessary to hire someone to mow the lawn. Anticipating the time challenges in advance helped the couple transition more easily into parenthood without unrealistic expectations that their current form of time management would remain the same.

Most of us are constantly rushing around, eating fast food, and working full days to pay for a lot of things we likely don't need. So, next time you think about time, think about what it costs you. You may be able to do things differently to create more free time for yourself (and I don't mean having more time for laundry, unless, of course, that's what makes you truly joyful).

Once your baby arrives, time becomes even more important. Identify how you're currently spending your time and how you could more effectively use your time to make sure you don't miss out on important moments. Because babies grow so quickly, you're reminded of time passing almost on a daily basis. On the other hand, the days can be quite long with a little one—all the feeding, changing, and playing. The key is to focus on the now and enjoy what's happening, as opposed to allowing time to slip away with thoughts of how little there is.

Don't forget to incorporate dinners out and "me" time into your time management plan. Even if you have a built-in babysitter nearby—like a good friend or a grandparent—you'll most likely want to be with baby once she arrives and you may feel a pull of guilt when you're not with her. But remember, "if mama ain't happy, then nobody's happy."

Implement Effective Household Systems

What's a system? It's a group of interrelated elements that form a functional whole. Systems allow us to effectively perform the same task over and over again without glitches. In fact, productivity rises when systems are put in place because we eventually know the system so well that we can accomplish our tasks more efficiently. Also, if you experience a chaotic day or week, getting back on track is easier if you have a system to return to because you already know how it works.

Systems are also valuable when you share a space with other people because if you're both following a system, it eliminates the "Where did you leave such and such?" and "I can't find the whatever." Setting up systems in your home will provide a way to accomplish daily tasks with ease and fluidity. In a busy household, the major systems to have in place include: mail, Family Communications Center, bill paying, laundry, grocery shopping, and cleaning. If these systems run effectively, they don't need to be considered drudgery. Instead, they're tasks that can easily be performed by almost anyone in the household. If someone is out of town, other family members can easily step in and take charge.

Put systems in place for routine tasks so you can focus efforts on what's most important. Family members can help out because you'll all know where items belong. The systems can be found in each chapter, including many in the Chapter 15, General Home Organization.

Problem—Solved!

Unfortunately, Linda never had systems in place. She felt that doing the same thing over and over again made one dull and rigid. Linda was proud of the fact that she was a free thinker and easygoing person. What she didn't realize was that, although she perceived herself that way, others perceived her as being scatterbrained and disorganized because she could never find anything. Paperwork began to pile up on her kitchen counter, becoming so overwhelming that it became too much to deal with—so Linda didn't deal with it at all.

Linda would try new organizing ideas, but never followed through long enough to implement a system and determine what was working and what wasn't. Her husband was frustrated and fearful that once the baby arrived, the disorganization and stress level would worsen. He was right.

Once the baby arrived, the mail often wouldn't even make it into the house. And if it did, it was typically in the diaper bag. Linda began to realize that the physical clutter was drastically affecting her emotional sanity. She then became open to her husband's idea of putting a system in place for handling the mail, especially the bills to be paid. They set up a portable file container with hanging folders labeled "Bills to Be Paid" and "Bills Paid," as well as individual files for each of them and an "Action" file for other mail that needed attention. So it didn't matter who brought in the mail; it always went in the same place.

02 | The Lowdown on Lingo

This chapter helps familiarize moms-to-be with new terms such as Binky, nesting, travel systems, Moses baskets; the difference between a carriage, stroller, and a pram; and more. We could provide a glossary of terms, but having this information upfront will get moms-to-be on the same page before moving through the book.

Before we go further, let's make sure we're speaking the same language. Now that you're expecting a baby, expect to learn a new language when it comes to equipment and accessories. What's the difference between a carriage, a stroller, and a pram? Thought they were all the same piece of equipment, didn't you? Here are some common terms defined.

- **baby carrier:** No, this isn't someone who carries your baby for you! A baby carrier is worn like a backpack, except on your chest, with baby tucked inside, facing you or facing out. It allows you to have your hands free but still have your baby close to you. With baby facing you, face-to-face interaction is also possible.
- **bassinet:** This is a small crib (usually smaller than a cradle), usually on wheels, with a hood over one end. They often come with bedding, or some decorations on them. Standard mattress size is 16" x 32".
- **bath ring:** This is a great tool for when baby is able to sit by himself, but you still want to have some support for him in the tub. It's a small seat that surrounds baby up to under his shoulders (depending upon baby's size) and keeps him from toppling over.
- **Bella Band:** This stretchy band fits around your waist and holds up your unbuttoned pre-pregnancy pants until you're ready for true

maternity pants. The band looks like it could be a layered shirt underneath the top you wear.

- **Binky:** A brand name for a pacifier, which is the nipple parents pop into a baby's mouth to help her soothe herself—and her parents.

- **bulb syringe:** A tool you can use to remove mucus from baby's nose to help him or her breathe easier when he or she is suffering from a stuffy nose. Also called a nasal aspirator.

- **carriage:** This piece of equipment has more features than a stroller and fewer than a pram. Typically, a carriage will allow baby to fully recline and provides a cozier, enclosed space for your newborn. The reversible handle will allow you to see baby while strolling or have baby facing forward.

- **convertible carseat:** So-named because it can be used as a rear-facing carseat for infants from 5 pounds up to 30 to 35 pounds, then converted into a forward-facing carseat for toddlers one year of age or older, and approximately 20 to 40 pounds.

- **co-sleeping:** Sleeping in close proximity to your child; also called "bed sharing." It can mean that the baby literally shares your bed, or that the baby sleeps in a separate mini-crib that you pull up to your bedside. This practice is controversial in the United States, but common in other countries. Check with the U.S. Consumer Product Safety Commission (CPSC) and the American Academy of Pediatrics (AAP) for more information.

- **cradle:** A small crib, usually on rockers. The standard mattress size is 18" x 36". It is larger than a bassinet but smaller than a regular crib.

- **diaper covers:** Used over cloth diapers to prevent wetness and leaking. They come in a variety of styles and materials.

- **diaper pail:** Unfortunately, a Diaper Genie is not someone who changes the baby's diapers in the middle of the night! It's a container for dirty diapers, along with brands such as Diaper Champ and Diaper

Dekor. They all keep the diaper's odor from being released into the nursery.

- **doula:** A nonmedical person who assists during labor and provides support to the mother, the infant, and the family after childbirth. She encourages using techniques learned in childbirth classes to avoid the use of an epidural and is often referred to as a labor assistant or coach. She does not deliver the baby, however.

- **infant carseat:** These are designed to support the back, head, and neck of a developing infant. They must be installed rear-facing in the back seat. Most will accommodate infants from 5 pounds up to 22 pounds (some accommodate up to 30 pounds), and many come with a base that stays in the car so you can lift the baby in and out in the carrier without disturbing him or her.

- **jogging stroller:** Specifically designed with bigger wheels for running and tough terrain. Do your research when purchasing one because when and where you use the stroller (for example, at the beach versus on woody trails) will make the difference in the features you need.

 good idea!
Visit a baby store near you to examine strollers in person. You get a much better sense of how big they are and can better judge which one is the best fit for you, your baby, and your space.

- **lactation consultant:** A person who educates and assists a new mom with breastfeeding her baby. Most hospitals have a lactation consultant on staff.

- **layette:** The formal French definition is the set of clothing and bedding for a newborn. For the purposes of this book, we'll define layette as the outfit of clothing, including a blanket, that the baby wears home from the hospital or the first few days after she is born when friends and family come to visit.

- **midwife:** A person, usually a woman, who is trained to birth and/or assist in childbirth and the delivery of babies. A midwife is trained to recognize and deal with abnormal situations, but generally doesn't intervene unless necessary. Some midwives are accredited and can help a woman deliver in the hospital or at home.

- **Moses basket:** A small bassinet that usually rests on the floor and is made of wicker material. Generally comes with padding inside the basket. For babies up to eighteen pounds. Great item for carrying baby around different parts of your home or yard.

- **nesting:** A period of time, usually in the third trimester, when a mom-to-be experiences a burst of energy and wants to organize her home to prepare for baby's arrival.

- **nursing pillow:** A pillow made for nursing moms—the popular Boppy brand comes in the shape of a crescent, while other types form a circle. While seated, you secure the pillow around your middle and lay baby across it for easier nursing and less strain on your arms and back. This pillow also works well on the floor to prop up babies before they can sit up effectively on their own. It's also a great head-rest for a tired parent lying on the floor while baby plays nearby. Many nursing pillows now come with removable and washable covers, which is handy in case baby spits up on it.

- **Onesie:** A one-piece undershirt that covers the baby's diaper and snaps at the bottom. Comes in short- or long-sleeve. Onesie is a brand name, but you can also find generic types as well.

- **pacifier:** A plastic or silicone nipple used to help soothe baby's sucking reflex. Also referred to as a Binky.

- **pram:** Generally an expensive, flat-bottomed, bulky carriage with a metal chassis. Not as practical as a carriage or stroller.

- **stationary entertainer:** An entertainer is a exerciser and entertainment center in one. It allows babies to sit, stand, bounce, and rock.

- **stroller:** A scaled-down carriage that provides little support and easily folds up for storage. Generally baby needs to be sitting up on her own to be comfortable in this piece of equipment. Great for travel and quick shopping trips.

- **swaddle:** Sometimes called the "burrito roll," swaddling is when you wrap a baby snugly in a blanket so she is not disturbed by her own startle reflex (which is what makes her arms and legs flail periodically while she sleeps). Swaddling also helps baby stay warm for the first few days until her internal thermostat kicks in.

- **travel system:** A set that includes a stroller and infant carseat. The infant carseat fits on top of the stroller so baby faces the person pushing the stroller. The carseat can also unsnap from the stroller and be placed into a small base that stays in the car. Once baby is big enough, she can sit directly in the stroller facing the same direction as the person pushing it (and you'll use a different type of carseat designed for bigger babies).

- **umbrella stroller:** This is a lightweight, collapsible stroller that's easy to use in tight spots. However, they're more comfortable for toddlers than infants because they don't provide as much support. It is smaller and more lightweight than a stroller or carriage.

 good idea!

Many moms- and dads-to-be assume they have to begin babyproofing as soon as they see the positive pregnancy test. While it's important to be sure your home is safe, babyproofing generally doesn't come into play until baby is mobile, which is typically around six months. So don't worry about running out while you're pregnant to lock up the cabinets and doors! You will also be better able to determine what needs to be babyproofed once baby begins to move.

03 | GOPACK 101:
The Step-by-Step Guide to Achieving Organizing Results

The GOPACK method takes you through a series of steps—Grouping Objects, Purging, Assigning, Containing, and Keeping It Up—to create an organized space or spaces. To create a positive experience and succeed at organizing, it's important to be prepared. Follow these steps to set yourself up for success. First, let's tackle a few fundamentals.

Understanding Zones

It's easier to understand how a particular room functions if you create zones. A zone is a particular space where a specific activity happens. It is an area that is distinguished from adjacent parts by a distinctive feature or characteristic. Zones help divide a room or space into usable sections and provide direction on where to store items for a particular task. (Kindergarten rooms are notorious for being zoned, which makes it easy for children to understand what happens in a particular area of the room.) It also helps you to decide where to place items. For example, in a nursery, you would place diapers in the "Changing" zone and clothing in the "Dressing" zone. It may sound remedial or elementary to talk about zoning your rooms like a kindergarten classroom, but the key to organizing is to make things as uncomplicated as possible. Keep this concept in mind as you work on the Map form (see next page).

What to Tackle First

Decide in advance your particular area of focus and how long you will spend during an organizing session. How do you decide? As a mom-to-be, the nursery is the place to begin. However, if you've already set up the nursery and are on to the next organizing project, go to the next most important area that you feel needs work.

Fill out the Map form to identify the area and estimate the amount of time you will need to devote to organizing it.

The Map Form

The Map form outlines the goal of the space and zones for the space. The form also outlines the steps you'll take to accomplish the project, including the task of donating items and collecting a tax receipt. There's also a place to record which containers you'll purchase and a way to keep up the systems by using the Keep It Up forms on pages 233–37. You'll fill out one Map form for each space you want to organize. You can use the blank forms shown on pages 238–42, or visit *www.stacey crew.com/pages/gopack.htm* to print out more.

How to Prepare

To prepare for what can be an emotionally and physically challenging project, get plenty of rest before you begin organizing. Start by taking an early morning walk, followed by a healthy breakfast to help you feel energized and ready to tackle the job. Keep snacks and plenty of water handy to avoid hunger and dehydration. Stop for a lunch break and for rest breaks at least five minutes every hour. Here are some guidelines that will keep you focused and on track to success:

- If you're organizing after the baby has been born, have your spouse take charge of the baby. Better yet, find a sitter and enlist the help of your spouse.

- Don't answer the telephone while you're organizing. This will unfocus you and make it more difficult to get back on track.
- Turn off the television.
- Put on some motivating music that will keep you moving through the process.
- Keep focused on the task at hand—the particular step in the method—and, as tempting as it may be, don't deviate from the plan.

How Long Will It Take?

It takes a long time to accumulate clutter and it will take time to declutter. Each situation is unique, so I can't estimate how long it will take you to do your specific project. Much, however, will depend upon how quickly you can make decisions. If you decide in advance that you won't keep anything that is broken, for example, purging will go a lot quicker. Establish some guidelines similar to those upfront to make the process go more quickly.

Work in three- to four-hour blocks. Record how much time it takes to GOPACK one area. Then, based on what you accomplish, you can more effectively estimate how much time it will take to GOPACK other areas. Keep in mind that certain areas, such as the kitchen, will take you longer because the kitchen typically contains a large number of items. Other areas that are typically jam-packed are children's rooms, craft rooms, and garages.

Don't Overdo It!

When you don't set limits, you end up worn out and overworked. That's why it's important to set time limits so you maintain your enthusiasm and stamina. In advance, determine how long you will work on a particular area. Ideally, you'll want to limit the organizing session to three or four hours. Remember to take breaks.

Break down the project into smaller pieces to make the project more manageable. It's easy to want to tackle an entire project in one day and keep going until it's done, but it's very important that you pace yourself! This is helpful for two reasons:

1. You don't want to reach a point where you're totally discouraged and give up on tackling the next part of the project.
2. You should take time to evaluate and enjoy what you've accomplished before proceeding to the next stage.

Also, throughout the three- to four-hour timeframe, constantly reassess the situation. You may determine that you underestimated or overestimated the amount of time it takes to perform a particular task.

Manageable Pieces

Break down the organizing project into manageable pieces by completing a Map form for each space you plan to organize. Doing so will help you prioritize where to begin. The Map form provides the details needed to effectively organize a space or spaces. If you're having trouble deciding where to begin, start with the space that raises your stress level the most when you enter it.

GOPACK Method

Put on some comfy clothes, and turn on your radio or iPod. Take a "before" picture so you can see visible results once you're done. Begin by taking your completed Map form to the room or area where you will work. You're ready to begin!

GOPACK is an acronym to help you remember the steps to getting organized (see table on the following page).

GOPACK Method

	ACTIONS	DECISIONS	RESULTS
	First step in getting results!	*You can do it!*	*This is what the GOPACK method is all about!*
Group **O**bjects	Group like items together into piles. Helpful hint: Use clear shoebox-like containers or Bankers Boxes to hold items temporarily. Label the containers/boxes!	None yet!	You'll know exactly what you have. For example, the seven rolls of tape that have accumulated because you couldn't find the last roll you used.
Purge	Decide whether to keep the item or give it away. Helpful hint: Tackle one pile/container at a time and decide whether you use it, love it, or want to make space for it.	Ask, "Does this serve me in my life today?" Be deliberate about your choices of what to keep and what to purge. Go to *www.staceycrew.com/ pages/gopack.htm* for a complete list of easy-toss items.	Your space will hold only those things that you love and use, which will raise your energy level.
Assign	Determine the best home for your item(s) according to the use. For example, place items in the associated zone.	Divide your home into activity/usage zones.	Everything will be where you need it when you need it. For example, your keys! This will save you enormous amounts of time each day.
Contain	Measure and decide on what to contain. Helpful hint: Choose containers that you love and that inspire you.	Now it's time to buy those containers.	The right containers not only "contain" like items, but they mean easy cleanup when items stray from their home.
Keep It Up	Organizing is a daily practice, not a one-time event. Helpful hint: Perform this task when your energy level is high.	Spend fifteen minutes each day to maintain the system.	As you progress with your new systems, you'll find that you'll have more *free* time to focus on what's most important to you!

Group Objects

For most people, this step is the most grueling stage of the organizing process. It's the process of pulling stuff out of closets, drawers, and piles and putting like items together.

What to Know Before You Begin

A benefit of Grouping is that you may discover items that have been lost or misplaced. It's important to stay focused, keep moving, and avoid taking more than a moment to decide which category the item will go in. Remember that this is simply the Grouping stage; you're not making any decisions, other than to put like items together—the Purge stage comes next.

Supplies Needed:

- Bankers Boxes
- Sticky notes or labels
- Pen or marker
- Staging area: A large, open floor space or large table to place the grouped items

Steps to Grouping

1. Clear a large area in the room you are working in. Either place labeled boxes in the area or leave sticky notes on the floor or table to indicate which pile is which. Leave space between piles because they will grow. As you begin to group, label each pile. Have sticky notes handy to make additional labels as new categories crop up. Labeling will help you save time so that you don't have to think each time you pick up an item. Simply place it in the appropriate pile.

2. Address one area of a room at a time and begin by grouping the obvious. For example, if you're starting in the kitchen, begin with

the countertops. Continue grouping and placing items in the labeled categories of the staging area.

3. Once you have all your items grouped, you'll want to load all of the piles into boxes (if you weren't using boxes already) that have tops, such as Bankers Boxes, which are available at any office supply store (you can also use boxes collected from a grocery store or retail store—just be sure to label them). It may be a few days or weeks before you're able to get to the Purge stage. If all the items are contained in stackable, labeled boxes, you can retrieve items easily when you're ready for the next step.

Remember: The labeled boxes are not a permanent solution. You'll want to plan the Purge step to occur soon, especially if the boxes contain paperwork or anything with a due date.

Tips for Grouping

- **Move quickly:** The quicker you group the objects, the faster this stage goes.
- **Work with a buddy:** I can't stress this enough. Having the support of another person simplifies the process and makes it go faster. Make sure you choose someone who is honest with you and helps you to achieve your ultimate goal. Many people have friends who will tell them what they need to do, but not actually help with the execution . . . or who don't see them through to the end. You want someone who will do both so you can make progress and achieve your goal! This is where the value of a professional organizer comes into play. They can use their expertise to help you achieve your organizing goals in a timely manner. The National Association of Professional Organizers (*www.napo.net*) has more than 4,000 members—visit its website to search for a professional organizer in your area.

Purge

The lack of purging is why many people have so much clutter. It's difficult to part with items. You ask yourself things like "What if I need this in the future?" Or, you tell yourself that you'll keep it "just in case." Check out the Tips for Purging section for suggestions on how to eliminate items that you're having trouble letting go of.

What to Know Before You Begin

Begin the Purge by throwing away the obvious into the trash bag. Discard papers that you no longer need, including expired coupons, old newspapers, or materials from events that have already taken place. For example, throw away birthday party invitations or programs from a play unless you're a scrapbook enthusiast; if so, then you'll need an extra container to temporarily store those items.

You'll also want to take this opportunity to review items that need to be repaired. If you still think you'll repair the items, put them all in one place and make a commitment to fix them. Decide on the length of time you'll give yourself to fix them. If you don't reach that goal, get rid of them. Chances are they're not that important to you. It's time to be strong and make decisions!

Here is some information about each of the four boxes:

- **Donate:** When it comes to donating, choose a charity that is close to your heart. During the Purge step, place any items you no longer need or want—and that are not suitable for consignment—in the Donate box.

- **Consign:** These are items that are still in good condition that you no longer need or want that you can sell to a consignment shop or on eBay or a similar website. This will help you pay for things you really want to buy. Check with your local consignment shop for consigning options and guidelines.

- **Go Home:** The "Go Home" box is for items that belong somewhere else. For example, socks found in the kitchen belong in this box.
- **Return:** The Return box is for items that belong to someone else—who doesn't live in your home—or items that need to be returned to a store. If you find that you borrow items or return items to a store on a regular basis, set up a permanent place to keep these items. You can also reassess your shopping habits. Are you consistently shopping for the sake of shopping? It may be time to take up a new hobby.

The idea here is to keep up the pace and assign items to the Keep, Donate, Consign, Go Home, Return, and trash categories. Continue attacking the piles until you've reached the timeframe you've scheduled for that organizing session, remembering to take a five- to ten-minute break every hour or so.

Supplies Needed
- Four large cardboard boxes (at least 16" × 28")
- Trash bag
- Labels that read "Donate," "Consign," "Go Home," and "Return"

Steps to Purging
1. Apply the labels to your four boxes. Use a trash bag for the trash.
2. Begin by taking out the Bankers Boxes used in the Group stage. Open a box and take out one item at a time and decide whether it goes in the Donate, Consign, Go Home, or Return boxes or the trash. If you decide to keep the item and it belongs in the space you're focusing on, put it back in the labeled Bankers Box. We'll talk about what to do with those items in the Assign stage.

3. Go through all of the boxes, one by one, making decisions on whether to put the item in Donate, Consign, Go Home, Return, or trash. Keep up the pace. Enjoy the fact that you are making progress!

4. Once you've performed the Purge on each labeled box, you can begin to consolidate the items in those boxes, relabeling as you go. For example, say you have a box labeled "knives" and another labeled "utensils." After eliminating the excess during the Purge, theoretically the boxes should be emptier. Therefore, more than one category can fit in a box and be relabeled "Utensils and Knives."

5. Put the boxes aside until you're ready to move on to the Assign stage.

Note: If you reach a point where the Donate, Consign, Go Home, and Return boxes are overflowing, empty that particular box into a large trash bag and make sure you label it! Place the bag in a temporary spot until it's time to clean up.

✳ good idea!

While you're clearing out clutter, think about how you accumulated it. Sometimes **clutter = indecision + other people's expectations of us.** Oftentimes, clutter accumulates because we *can't* decide what to do with the item, so it stays where it's been placed (decision-making requires focus, intent, and follow-through). "Other people's expectations" refers to, say, home parties (for example, selling jewelry, kitchen items, etc.): The hostess invites you with the expectation of you buying something. You don't really need or want anything, but feel obligated. Result: You wind up with something you don't need or want and perhaps no place to store it. The better you know your clutter-accumulating habits, the better you can stop them.

Tips for Purging

- **Go with your gut:** If you think you won't use it, you probably won't. Put it in Donate, Consign, or the trash.

- **Keep it simple:** Avoid telling yourself that you should make individual piles for particular people. Place the items to be donated and returned in their separate boxes, invite friends and family over to look in the boxes, and let them take what they'd like from Donate and pick up anything that's theirs from Returns. Attach a time limit to the donations offer.

- **Be realistic:** If you haven't used an item in the past year, you probably won't.

- **Don't save every piece of paperwork:** Research says that 80 percent of the paper you file will never be accessed again. If the paperwork falls under the category of memorabilia, treat it as a treasured item and file it as such.

- **Work with a buddy:** If you're having trouble parting with items, consult with your buddy during the Purge. If you're looking at a piece of clothing, for example, that you think you might wear again, ask your buddy for an honest opinion. She may tell you it makes you look older than your years, and that it's time to get rid of it!

- **Be honest with yourself:** Just because your aunt gave you a set of coasters doesn't mean that you have to display them. Give them to someone who would like them in his or her house. If you feel emotionally obligated to display them when your aunt comes to visit, put the coasters (and other items that fall into the same category) into a box that sits on a shelf in the garage, and take them out only when your aunt visits; put them away after the visit. There's nothing worse than staring at the item every day if it depletes your energy.

- **Pace yourself:** Remember to take sufficient breaks throughout each stage of the process. Eat snacks and stay hydrated.

Assign

Now that you've eliminated all the items you no longer need or want, it is time to focus on what you've decided to keep.

What to Know Before You Begin

The Assign stage is a time to revisit your map and decide where to place categories of items. Your Map form contains the designated zones, so you're already on your way.

Supplies Needed

- Paper
- Pencil and eraser

 good idea!
If you're beginning to feel overly emotional, stop and regroup. Go back to the Purge when your energy level returns and you're prepared to make decisions. The Purge stage is all about making decisions and this will likely take a lot of energy.

Steps to Assigning

1. Draw the space on the piece of paper. If you're working in a room, draw a floor plan. If you're working in a closet, draw the elevation. Use a tape measure to add the dimensions.

2. Next, draw in the pieces of furniture and equipment. Be sure to include everything you plan to keep in the space. Be sure to leave approximately 20 percent clear space in any container so you have room to grow.

3. Physically move the furniture into position after you've carefully considered all of the components.

4. Next, look at the labels on the boxes and place the boxes in the appropriate zone within the space.

5. Open the boxes and look at the exact space where you will place the items to determine whether they'll fit. If you haven't allotted enough space, see if you can eliminate another category in another location or downsize what you're containing.

Tips for Assigning

- **Keep items where you use them:** There's no sense in keeping the vacuum cleaner in the basement if you use it on the first floor.
- **Think of spaces within spaces:** Contain small items such as paperclips and staples in smaller containers within a drawer space.
- **Keep like items together.**
- **Eliminate duplicates:** Though you've likely taken care of this during the Purge, keep an eye out during this stage for anything that slipped through the cracks.
- **Special projects:** If you're working on a temporary project that needs to be transported outside the home, use portable containers and find a parking space for the containers in an out-of-the-way area in your home or office. One example would be "Baby Nursery," where you would need a container to hold magazine articles; pictures of cribs, dressers, and so forth; paint chip possibilities; fabric samples; and receipts from items purchased. Another example may be "Landscaping," for improvements you're planning for your yard. In that folder, you could place ideas, designs, quotes from contractors, a wish list, etc.

Contain

Containing is the process of giving things a permanent home. A container is anything that holds something else.

What You Need to Know Before You Begin

Containers come in all shapes and sizes. For example, a coffee table with drawers is a container, a filing cabinet is a container for files, and a kitchen cabinet is a container for dishes. Containing helps you achieve the ultimate goal of organizing—it gives you a place for everything. Finding containers doesn't have to be expensive or complicated. Empty shoeboxes that are labeled work just as well as an expensive box from a fancy store.

 good idea!

Contain items in appropriately sized, environmentally friendly containers. Organize.com has an entire "green" section offering these options—check out their selection.

Supplies Needed

- Tape measure
- Label machine or permanent marker
- Map form to record container quantities, sizes, and descriptions

Steps to Containerizing

1. Measure the piles that you plan to place in the container and always leave at least 20 percent more room for the items to grow.
2. Measure the spaces where you will place containers.
3. Record the quantities, sizes, and descriptions on the Map form.
4. Purchase the containers.

5. Label the containers, if necessary. You usually want to label containers, but in some cases—for example, an under-the-sink organizer—you can skip this step. And keep in mind that kitchen cabinets or bathroom vanities *are* containers, but there's likely no need to label them, so simply move on to Step 6.

6. Load the items into their new home.

Tips for Containing

- **Choose wisely.** If your budget allows, choose containers that reflect your personality and make you feel good. Even if budget is a concern, numerous options and price points are available (see Appendix B).

- **Use containers that are consistent in shape, color, and size.** The eye finds it easier to process what it is seeing when the containers are consistent (shoeboxes covered in gift wrap from a discount store work well).

- **Label everything.** This is the best way to ensure items will find their way home. It makes the systems easier for you—and others—to maintain because the label immediately identifies what lives in that container.

Keep It Up

Once you've finished the first four steps of the process, you'll need to maintain your organized home regularly.

What to Know Before You Begin

The Keep It Up forms help you determine what needs to be done on a daily, weekly, monthly, semiannual, and annual basis. Fill out the forms and post them on the refrigerator or in the Family Communications Center area (see Chapter 15, General Home Organization, for the complete family communications system).

- **Daily Keep It Up** tasks include picking up coats and shoes, putting away toys and books, emptying and loading the dishwasher, and putting dirty laundry in the laundry sorter.
- **Weekly Keep It Up** tasks include putting out the recycling for pickup, changing bedding, and washing towels.
- **Monthly Keep It Up** tasks might include dropping off the items in your Donate container.
- **Semiannual Keep It Up** tasks might include changing smoke detector batteries.
- **Annual Keep It Up** tasks might include cleaning out and organizing the garage or trimming the hedges.

Supplies Needed

❑ Keep It Up forms (see pages 233–37)

Steps to Keep It Up

1. Take fifteen minutes a day to clear counters, desktops, and so on, sending items to their appropriate homes.
2. Reward yourself by relaxing in whatever way you like.

Tips to Keep It Up

- Enlist the help of family members to help during an assigned fifteen-minute period each day.
- Purge on a regular basis.
- If you take it out, put it back.
- When it comes to paper, keep in mind that you'll probably never look at 80 percent of what you file.

Staying Motivated

Although organizing can be emotionally and physically challenging, keep in mind that you'll have clarity and peace of mind when you reach your organizing goals. Eliminate the unnecessary distractions in your space, and you'll be free to focus on the fun stuff.

Here are a few suggestions for staying motivated during your organizing project:

- Focus on the big picture by remembering why you decided to get organized.
- Avoid negative people while you are completing the project. A naysayer will only provide reasons why something can't be accomplished versus why it can or how he can help.
- Talk to your buddy about how you feel and ask her for a pep talk to keep you going. Sharing how you feel with a supportive friend will help to keep you motivated.
- Reward yourself for the incremental accomplishments you make. Treat yourself to your favorite restaurant—or better yet, a massage.
- Listen to your favorite music or go out for a walk or a run. Take a break and enjoy your favorite activity.

Approach organizing as you would any other project that has time-lines and deadlines. Use the schedule forms in the back of the book to set your goal dates and check off your achievements. Post this where you can see it regularly so you can congratulate yourself on a job well done. Most of all, give yourself credit for the milestones you reach!

Completing the Job

Supplies Needed
❑ General cleaning supplies: Paper towels, surface cleaner, dust cloth

Steps to Completing the Project

1. Place the trash and the Donate, Consign, Go Home, and Return boxes in the appropriate destinations: Immediately put the trash items in the trash can. The Go Home items will need to be put back in the appropriate area (for example, a toothbrush belongs in the bathroom, not the kitchen). Finally, load the Donate, Consign, and Return boxes into your car or arrange to have them picked up.

2. Clean the area by dusting and vacuuming. This is also a good time to open windows and allow some fresh air to clear out any stagnant energy that has accumulated with the clutter.

3. When you're ready to stop for the day, begin cleaning up at least thirty minutes prior to the stop time. Collect the trash and put away your supplies.

4. Congratulate yourself on a job well done! Sit back and enjoy your organized space.

5. Take "after" pictures to give you a true sense of accomplishment.

Reward Yourself!

Don't forget to follow through on the reward listed on your Map form. This is important! Although organizing in itself can bring overall satisfaction, the process can be emotionally draining. The reward system helps you stop and consciously celebrate your success.

Plan in advance the reward for yourself once you've completed an area. Whatever it is, be sure that the reward is set up in advance. That way you don't have to exert a lot of energy determining what the reward is, and you'll know what you have to look forward to.

Now that you have an overview of the key areas of organization, we will move to one of the most fun and important chapters in organizing for your new baby: creating a home for your bundle of joy.

04 | Organizing the Nursery

Toward the end of pregnancy, most moms-to-be experience what is called the "nesting stage," defined as a sudden burst of energy a pregnant woman has that motivates her to clean and organize before baby arrives. It's nature's gift to the mom-to-be to help her prepare for baby's arrival.

When furnishing a nursery, many focus simply on the aesthetic aspects of a nursery (what color to paint the walls, for example) without much consideration of the functional aspects, which are equally, if not most, important. *The Organized Mom* takes the top-down approach for creating a clear vision of what she wants. She begins by choosing colors and textures, but quickly defines zones for specific activities and functions (for example, sleeping, changing, dressing, and playing), which brings it all together. That's what we'll discuss in this chapter.

Problem—Solved!

Debbie was not what you would call an organized person. She regularly misplaced her car keys; occasionally she would receive a call notifying her that her car payment was late, which occurred because the bills wound up at the bottom of a stack of papers. Routinely, Debbie arrived late to events. She couldn't be counted on to RSVP to a party. If she showed up, it was only because she remembered at the last minute. Therefore, when Debbie and her husband decided to have a baby, the thought of setting up the nursery in the current guest room, which really looked like a storage room, was overwhelming.

Debbie and Robby called in an organizer to help them get started. The organizer helped them create a vision for the room, as well as a focal point and a plan for how the furniture and accessories would be placed in the nursery—the "big picture" of the room.

Next, in order to clear the room and store the sporting equipment and extra furniture that currently resided in the space, the organizer helped them group objects together, purge what was no longer needed—which was a lot—and relocate what they were keeping to other areas of the home (attic and garage mainly). The result was a calm and restful, yet functional space, for the new baby.

The Early Days of the Nursery

In reality, during the first few weeks of baby's life, the nursery gets used very little. Typically, after baby arrives home, mom will spend a good bit of time in the comfort of her own bed recovering from the physical stresses of childbirth, and may choose to let the baby sleep nearby in a bassinet or portable crib. This gives the mom an opportunity to recover and do nighttime feedings without having to trek to the nursery. As a new mom, you can easily become exhausted if you do not get adequate rest during the first couple of weeks after baby is born. It's a tricky time because you're also attempting to establish a routine for baby.

Initially, the nursery is a place of restful existence for your little one . . . and you. Consider adding a rocker or comfortable chair for nursing, feedings, or reading. Music is an important part of a baby's development, too. Set up a CD or MP3 player with a speaker so you can easily switch on music day or night. Studies show that music stimulates brain growth in babies. Remember, babies take their cues from mom—when mom is calm, so is baby.

With all that in mind, don't be terribly concerned with completing the nursery setup before baby arrives. Having the room painted, the furniture placed, and the necessary items on hand for baby is most important.

The final decorations and toys will come later—and, trust me, there will be lots of gifts in the way of toys and decorative items for the nursery.

Let's begin with creating a vision for the space, then move on to determining a focal point and defining specific zones in the space. We'll finish up the chapter with organizing baby's closet, additional ways to make the nursery a great place to spend time, and creating baby zones in other parts of your home.

Creating a Clear Vision for the Nursery

You may have a vision of how the nursery will look and feel. If you do, that's great. However, if you need some inspiration and are unsure how you want the nursery to look and feel, this process will help.

First, gather some magazines and catalogs that contain nursery photos. If you don't have any magazines with nursery photos, regular home magazines will work just fine. As you look through the various publications, pull out the pictures that catch your eye. At this stage, don't worry about looking for a definitive picture of a nursery, you simply want to focus on pictures that appeal to you based on color and style.

Now that you've gathered pictures, cut them out and make a collage. It may sound remedial, but a theme will emerge containing the details we mentioned earlier: color, style, accessories, and furniture. You will discover a theme of colors, as well as the style and type of accessories that draw your attention to an overall theme. Next, based on the collage, list the following details that have emerged from your choices:

- Color and textures
- Style (contemporary, traditional, eclectic)
- Accessories (lamps, fan or light fixture, clock, bookshelf)
- Furniture items (crib, rocker, dresser, changing table)

Use these details when you shop and make choices for the nursery.

Problem—Solved!

Mary surprised herself when creating a vision for the nursery. She never considered herself to be "traditional" in style, and she wanted the nursery to be different and unique. However, as she gathered pictures that attracted her eye in magazines and catalogs, she gravitated toward traditional pieces of furniture, color schemes, and accessories. The initial inspiration for the nursery came from a piece of fabric that Mary obtained at a local fabric shop, which she used for the baby's bedding. The baby's grandpa, who is an artist, painted a mural on one wall. In the end, Mary wound up with something completely unexpected and personalized.

Other Considerations

When choosing a theme for the nursery, consider how long baby will occupy the room and how long you plan on living in the home. Those factors may determine whether it would be too costly to go with an infant theme versus using colors and furnishings that could easily transition to a preschool- or elementary school–aged child.

If you plan to have baby transition from infant to toddler in the same room, consider colors and furniture that would also suit a toddler. The frantic pace of life will quickly kick in, and eliminating the need to paint for perhaps years will help tremendously. Also, choose a kid-friendly type of paint, one that you can easily wash down with a wet cloth.

Give some thought to the room's characteristics—for example, the overall shape and the position of the windows and doorways. Also take into account whether a focal point already exists—for instance, a beautiful view out the windows. Address the lighting situation too: Do you need to install an overhead light or does one already exist? What type of indirect lighting will you use? With many of these issues addressed, you'll really have the neurons popping so you can come up with something terrific!

Nailing Down a Theme

After you've chosen colors, textures, and styles, you'll likely decide on a theme as well. It could be as simple as trains or geometrical shapes. Or, you may have a family heirloom that dictates the direction. Make it meaningful and personal. You may want to wait until baby arrives and his or her personality begins to emerge before you add theme-related items.

What You Need

❑ Baby monitor   ❑ Crib and bedding

❑ Books/toys   ❑ Dresser

❑ Changing table   ❑ Hamper

❑ Cradle*   ❑ Humidifier*

❑ Mobile* for over the crib or changing table (Be sure to remove this once your child is sitting up and can reach it and potentially pull it down. This happens at around five months.)

❑ Moses basket*

❑ Music player (CD or MP3)

❑ Nightlight (great for middle of the night so you don't have to turn on the overhead light, keeping baby from fully waking up)

❑ Ottoman*

❑ Pack-n-Play*

❑ Rocking chair/Glider*

❑ Storage

❑ Trash can

*Nice, but not necessary (check with your pediatrician on the humidifier).

Where to Put It

❑ We'll talk about where to put certain items over the course of this chapter.

Space Planning 101

Space planning involves making several considerations upfront, beginning with an evaluation of the space. Two overall components go into space planning a room:

1. **Decorative** consists of the paint color, flooring, furniture choices, and accessories.
2. **Functional** includes how you use the space and how things are organized within the space.

Effective space planning improves any room, but this is especially so in a nursery because there are many functions that take place in this one space: sleeping, changing/dressing, playing, reading, and rocking.

 good idea!
For additional storage, use an under-the-bed container hidden by a dust ruffle on the crib to store extra blankets or toys. Some crib manufacturers now offer a built-in drawer under the crib so you can skip the dust ruffle and gain storage.

Determining the Focal Point

In order to create a functional yet pleasing-to-the-eye space, you'll want to choose a focal point for the room. Generally, the focal point is the first thing you see when you enter the space. In a nursery, the crib is typically the focal point. It's best to keep the changing table out of your direct line of sight as you enter the room, so if you are changing baby and someone else enters the room they're not presented with baby's bottom. Just a thought.

If possible, place the changing table against a solid wall as opposed to kitty-corner so you can hang a shelf above it to place items you need

to have handy. Also consider hanging a mobile from the ceiling above the changing table so baby has something to focus on while you're changing her diaper. If that's not possible, have a couple of small toys handy for your baby to hold to prevent her putting her hands in the diaper while it's being removed. It's a natural movement for baby to pull her knees to her chest, place a hand in between, and touch her bottom.

If space permits, consider setting up a rocking chair or glider with a small end table next to it for a place to rest a bottle or glass of water. Remember to stay hydrated!

Defining Zones in the Nursery

Kids love organization! If they can easily identify where an item goes, they can also easily help clean up. Granted, this comes later—but even children as young as a year can learn to put things away in their proper places given simple direction.

- **Sleeping**—You could place an armoire or chest near the crib with extra blankets or bedding. Consider zoning a portion of the closet to contain extra bedding if floor space in the room is limited. For extra storage, use containers that slide under the crib—covered by a dust ruffle, no one will know and you will be maximizing space.

- **Changing**—The changing table and all related supplies go in this zone. It's best to have closed storage below so that when baby begins crawling and exploring, she isn't emptying the supplies that are housed underneath. Consider adding a sturdy shelf above the changing table (out of baby's reach but within yours) for other supplies.

- **Clothing/Storage**—Place the dresser and/or closet in this zone. Separate and organize clothing by category. For example, socks and pajamas in one drawer, shirts in another, bottoms in another. Store only current-sized clothing in the dresser. Use the clothing system (see page 51) to store sizes baby hasn't grown into yet . . . or has already grown out of.

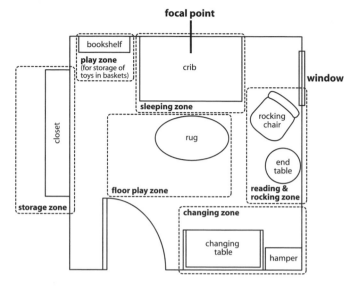

Nursery zones.

Labels in figure:
focal point
bookshelf
play zone (for storage of toys in baskets)
crib
window
closet
sleeping zone
rocking chair
rug
end table
floor play zone
reading & rocking zone
storage zone
changing zone
changing table
hamper

- **Play**—Books and toys go in this zone. Ideally, a bookshelf—secured to the wall—provides ample storage. Use the top shelves for collectibles and delicate items and the bottom shelves for toys, books, and other items that are safe for baby to touch.
- **Reading and Rocking**—Place rocker or glider here.
- **Floor Play**—Rug and floor space where you and baby can play.

Floor Plan Exercise

It may be useful to draw out a floor plan on paper, including doorways, windows, and closet location. This doesn't have to be an architectural-quality drawing by any means; it's simply an illustration to help you gauge what you can actually fit in the room and where it will go. If you want to get more specific, use graph paper to sketch out the drawing after you have measured the space, representing 1 foot per square.

After you've made the initial rough diagram of the space, make a short list of the large pieces of furniture you intend to place in the room.

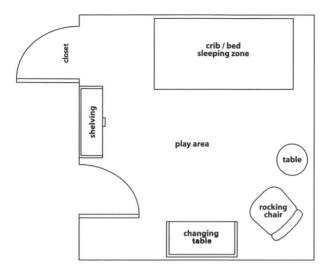

Sample nursery layout.

For example: crib, changing table, and rocker. Take another sheet of paper and cut out pieces of paper that resemble each piece of furniture and place them on the layout. (Again, if you want to get specific about the furniture size versus approximating, measure the furniture pieces and use graph paper to cut out the appropriate sizes.) Move the cutouts around the diagram until the placement feels right.

good idea!

Consider installing a dimmer switch on the overhead light in the nursery. It will be convenient for evening and middle-of-the-night changes/feedings.

Once you've determined on paper the furniture layout, physically move the furniture into place. The floor plan exercise will save you the time and energy needed to physically move the furniture from place to place until you get it right.

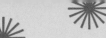

Space Planning the Closet

Many closet spaces are underutilized. For example, vertical space, if planned well, can truly maximize the entire closet real estate. To really make the most of closet storage, install shelving at the top of the closet for non-everyday items (perhaps seasonal storage), midlevel shelving for hanging items and supplies, and lower shelving for baskets of toys.

Here's how to plan out the nursery closet:

1. Draw a rough picture of the closet (an outline of it, looking at it straight on) using a piece of plain white paper.
2. Determine the zones in the space—clothing, toys, keepsakes, hamper, books, and so on.
3. Determine your shelving and hanging needs, then purchase and install them.
4. Load closet, placing items in predetermined zones. Use baskets or bins to contain toys and miscellaneous supplies (for example, extra diapers or shampoo).

Tips for Planning a Nursery Closet

- If you have enough room in the closet for hanging items, organize clothing by size and use dividers to easily identify those sizes.

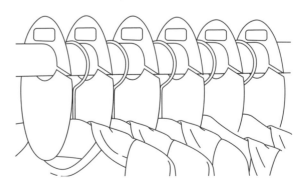

Size dividers help keep baby clothes organized.

- One way to gain vertical space in your closet without installing shelving is to add canvas bags that hang on existing rods. This will allow you to use the space below the hanging clothing to house folded items. Remember, baby clothing is small and doesn't take up much space. Avoid using a rod that extends the full length of the closet. Instead, double up on the rod space by installing one over the other and then install shelving on the unused side for baskets that hold extra baby supplies, toys, etc.

*A functional
baby closet.*

- Use the top shelves to store containers full of keepsakes and out-of-season clothes or clothes that baby hasn't grown into yet. Remember to label the containers. Also use the top shelves for other items not needed on a regular basis.

- Remember: Determine what will go in each container prior to choosing or purchasing the containers. Allow space to grow.

Problem—Solved!

Once her baby arrived, Abby was inundated with baby clothing up to size eighteen months. The closet was jam-packed—there was barely enough room for what baby currently fit into! Abby's friend, who had been down the road of having twins, came to her rescue. They spent a morning removing everything from the closet, storing the clothing in labeled containers that baby would grow into, and putting back only what baby was currently wearing. Once this was completed, there was room for storage of extra diapers, wipes, toys, and even a laundry basket. The storage containers were placed in another closet where they were easily accessible, but out of the way.

Pulling It All Together

To summarize, here is the sequence of events you should follow to organize and decorate the nursery:

1. **Create a vision** for the space by determining the color, textures, style, accessories, and furniture items.
2. **Determine the furniture** for the room—crib, changing table, rocker, dresser, and so forth.
3. **Choose a focal point**—the focal point is usually the first wall you see as you enter the space and the piece that is usually placed on this wall is the crib.

4. **Determine the theme**, if any.

5. **Space-plan the closet** and install any necessary closet organizers.

6. **Choose the paint color**, fabrics for drapes (or choose premade curtains), and bedding. Choosing the theme may drive the décor of the room. If this is the case, do Step 4 before Step 1. Choose a wall color and coordinating fabric and flooring. The flooring will most likely already be in place, but consider an area rug or throw rugs to match the décor. For a more economic solution in lieu of custom bedding or window treatments, consider stock bedding that fits your style.

7. **Paint the room.**

8. **Place the furniture.**

Organizing System for Baby and Children's Clothing

Organizing your baby's clothes is a subproject within the nursery. Infant clothing is a challenge because little ones grow so quickly.

Buy Containers First

Yes, this violates my don't-contain-til-you-know-how-much-you-have rule. But the reality is that you won't have much free time to shop for containers after the baby is born, and you will likely get gifts before baby is born anyway. So purchase some deep, clear containers—at least three—label them 0–3 months, 3–6 months, and 6–12 months. Another option, especially if pressed for storage space, is Space Bags, which allow you to suck out the extra air to save space. Always have at least three containers on hand through the two- or three-years mark, and you'll be able to store and easily locate clothing.

Label all containers! Storing clothes in labeled containers will make it easy when it comes time to loan, consign, or donate the items—they'll already be sorted! All you'll need to do is separate them by season. Once your baby has grown out of a size, you'll have a place to put them for storage, for the next child, for consignment, or to loan to a friend.

Storing the Clothes

If you receive clothes before the baby is born, remove the tags and wash all the clothing in a baby-friendly detergent. Then place the newborn or 0–3 month items in the baby's dresser and/or closet and put everything else in the labeled containers. Then when your infant begins to grow out of the 0–3 month clothing, place it in the 0–3 month container and place the 3–6 month clothing in closets and drawers.

As your child outgrows clothing, you may want to consider storing it separated by size *and* gender. For example, if you did not know the sex of your baby before he or she was born, you likely received neutral-colored clothing pre-birth, then gender-specific colors after his or her arrival. If you plan to have more children, separating the neutral 0–3 months clothes from the pink or blue 0–3 month clothes means that you can easily pull what you need when the next baby arrives. Having it separated by gender makes the donation/consignment/giveaway process much easier, and it creates less clutter because you only have to pull out what you need.

 good idea!

Don't overbuy, especially in advance. You may find that the cute little outfits with all the buttons and added trim just aren't practical, and baby will probably grow out of most of them before she has a chance to wear them. Don't forget that you'll also receive lots of gifts. You may also wind up choosing favorites due to the ease of wash-and-wear and style.

Stocking Up for Baby

As you prepare for baby's arrival, you will need to stock up on clothing, accessories, and linens, which will help avoid the task of laundry on a daily basis. Here are checklists of what clothing is helpful to have on hand.

What Baby Needs: Clothing

- ❏ 6 to 8 Onesies (one-piece garments that cover baby's body and snap between the legs—buy three or four in size 0–3 months and three or four in size 3–6 months)
- ❏ 2 to 4 rompers (one-piece, easy-to-wear outfits)
- ❏ 2 to 4 pairs of mittens (so baby does not scratch himself; socks are a great substitution)
- ❏ 1 to 2 two-piece outfits
- ❏ 4 to 6 sleepsacks (or pajamas)
- ❏ 2 to 4 caps/hats (appropriate for the season)
- ❏ 3 to 6 pairs of socks
- ❏ 1 cardigan sweater
- ❏ 2 diaper covers (if you're using cloth diapers)

---

 bonding with baby

Rocking your baby is a wonderful way to bond. Add an ottoman and a side table, and you're all set! Place a drink for yourself on the side table. Remember, if you're breastfeeding, drink at least one 8-ounce glass of water before each feeding. Even if you're not breastfeeding, drink at least eight glasses of water a day to stay hydrated.

What You Need: Bottle-feeding Items

- ❏ 4 to 6 four-ounce bottles
- ❏ 6 to 8 eight-ounce bottles
- ❏ Bottle warmer*
- ❏ 6 to 8 bibs
- ❏ Formula (discuss which type with your pediatrician)

* Nice, but not necessary.

What You Need: Breastfeeding Items

- ❏ Breast pads (they come in disposable or washable varieties—if you plan to breastfeed for a long time, you may want to consider washable pads, which can go in a mesh bag in the washing machine, then air dry)
- ❏ Breast pump* (might be a necessity if you plan to breastfeed for a long period of time)
- ❏ Nipple cream
- ❏ 3 nursing bras
- ❏ Nursing cover/wrap* (to give you and baby privacy if you need to nurse in the company of others)
- ❏ Nursing pillow (try a Boppy)
- ❏ Storage bottle set; along with storage bags if you intend to freeze milk

* Nice, but not necessary.

 good idea!
Drink a glass of water before each trip to the bathroom. This is a good way to stay on top of getting the necessary intake you need daily.

What You Need for an Infant Born in Warm-Weather Months

❑ 1 or 2 sunhats

❑ Sunscreen (make sure it's made especially for baby, and keep in mind that the American Academy of Pediatrics suggests that it's best to keep babies under six months out of the sun altogether)

What You Need for a Baby Born in Cold-Weather Months

❑ 1 snowsuit, bunting, or BundleMe carseat cover

❑ 1 pair of mittens

❑ 1 cap with earflaps

What You Need If You Choose Cloth Diapers

❑ 3 or 4 dozen diapers

❑ 7 or 8 moisture-proof, Velcro diaper covers

❑ 1 diaper pail, with lid

❑ Alternatively, you can call a diaper service, which will deliver clean diapers and pick up the soiled diapers for you generally once a week.

 good idea!

For the first few months, newborns will go through ten to twelve diapers per day, or seventy to eighty-four per week. After that, expect about eight per day, or fifty-six per week. Be sure you have enough on hand!

Setting Up the Changing Station

You've already chosen a piece of furniture for this task and probably have space available for the items you'll need within reach. Here's a list.

What You Need
❏ Diapers (10 to 12 per day for infants; may vary depending upon the baby)
❏ Wipes (use a container that allows you to easily open and grab a wipe with one hand)
❏ 1 changing pad and 2 to 3 covers for the changing table
❏ Diaper rash ointment
❏ Small pair of scissors (always handy to clip tags off new clothing)
❏ Brush and comb set
❏ Cotton balls or pads to clean the umbilical cord area
❏ Bulb syringe (to help clear out a baby's stuffed or runny nose)
❏ Thermometer
❏ Vaseline (used to heal a circumcision)
❏ Q-tips
❏ Cotton balls
❏ Diaper Genie or other diaper pail
❏ A toy to keep baby occupied during changing
❏ Fever-reducer and plastic syringe

 good idea!

When you need to give baby some fever-reducer, be prepared with a damp washcloth handy in case any dribbles out of the baby's mouth. Prop up baby's head, place the washcloth under baby's neck, and, using the plastic syringe, administer the medicine.

Where to Put It

❑ If you don't have a changing table with a drawer or shelves, attach a shelf to the wall next to or above the table, or hang a basket from the side of the table.

❑ There are many ways to store the items you need at a changing station. If your changing station is attached to a dresser, for example, you can use the top drawer to house all the necessary items. Place smaller items separately within the drawer in easy-to-open containers. For example, the Vaseline, fever-reducer, and rubbing alcohol can go in one container (in the event something spills, it won't get all over the other items in the drawer). Place dry items, such as cotton balls, Q-tips, and gauze in another container. Place these items in a basket or container nearby:

- Gas drops (speak to your pediatrician if you think your baby might need these)
- Liquid aspirin substitute (acetaminophen or ibuprofen)
- Antiseptic cream
- Hydrogen peroxide
- Band-Aids
- Tweezers
- Baby nail clippers

 memories and music

Set up a CD or MP3 player and listen to your favorite music with your baby. Hold your baby and sing to her. The nice part about singing to baby is that even if you don't have the greatest singing voice—like me—she won't know the difference! Both you and baby will have fond memories of those moments.

Burpcloths

You can never have enough burp cloths! Granted, burpcloths purchased in bulk typically aren't the most attractive, but they are extremely useful. Luckily, many companies on the market today offer burpcloths with monogramming and pretty trim.

Some additional uses for traditional burpcloths:

- Carry one in your diaper bag to use as a changing pad
- Sew on a ribbon and monogram for a custom look (makes a great gift, too!)
- Use it as a cushion between baby and the potentially cold travel changing pad (it'll provide a soft surface for baby and keeps the pad from getting dirty)
- Little girls love to use these as blankets for their baby dolls
- Later on, they make great dust rags

The Portable Changing Station

To avoid a long trek to the nursery every time baby needs a diaper change, set up a portable changing station in another location where you spend a lot of time. For example, if you live in a two-story house and the nursery is upstairs, consider a portable changing station downstairs in the family room.

 good idea!

After placing baby on the changing table, get in the habit of strapping your baby in from the start. That way, when she unexpectedly rolls over one day, she doesn't topple off the table. Even if you think your baby isn't at that stage yet, she may suddenly surprise you. Better safe than sorry in this situation.

Place a container (something with a handle so it's easy to pick up and move—there are many "portable changing station" containers on the market today) with a changing pad, diapers, wipes, and ointment. Add a blanket and a couple of toys to the basket so if you decide to spend a little time in another room, you can easily grab the basket, lay down the blanket, and put baby on it.

05 | Organizing the Kitchen

The kitchen takes on a new meaning once baby arrives, since you'll need a whole new array of tools to feed baby. Therefore, creating baby zones is critical in keeping counters clear and to easily put your hands on what you need.

For overall kitchen organization, divide and conquer. Typically, most kitchens are designed with the traditional "work triangle" in mind. A work triangle is an uninterrupted traffic pattern where the stove, sink, and refrigerator are positioned on different sides of a triangular pattern and are no more than nine feet apart. For purposes of this organization book, we will assume that your kitchen has the traditional work triangle. For organization purposes, the kitchen consists of five zones: Food Preparation, Cooking, Cleaning, Serving, and Food Storage. With your new addition, you'll want to add a sixth zone: baby. Later on, consider incorporating an Arts and Crafts zone where you store paper, crayons, washable markers, and coloring books so while you're preparing a meal, your little one can entertain himself.

This chapter provides specific organizing suggestions and systems to create space for the baby items that could otherwise wind up hogging precious countertop space. The suggestions include where to put everything from bottles to baby food to sippy cups. You'll also find meal-planning solutions to save time and make sure everyone gets proper nutrition during the frenetic time of having a new baby.

Problem—Solved!

When Martha and her husband found out they were having a baby, her sister told her that it was going to be a challenge for them to store all the supplies in their tiny city apartment. Martha began to assess her kitchen space, using the GOPACK method to reorganize. She added a baby zone to her plan for bottles, formula, baby food, bibs, and dishes. She dedicated one shelf in the pantry closet for baby, which worked out well. She went further and purchased clear containers to subdivide and label the items so when her mom came to help with the baby, she would know where to find everything.

What You Need in the Kitchen for Baby

- ❑ High chair (more on this shortly)
- ❑ Basket for clean bottles
- ❑ Dishwasher basket for baby items
- ❑ Separate container for bottle nipples so you can easily access them
- ❑ Small container for pacifiers
- ❑ Separate container in the utensil drawer for baby's utensils (small spoons when they begin eating solid food)
- ❑ Double lazy Susan for jars of baby food (this will maximize space and allow you to easily see what you have on hand)

High Chair

You probably won't use a high chair until baby begins to eat solids. Look for a reclining one with a padded cushion, so you can actually use the high chair when you do begin feeding baby solids, instead of waiting until she is sitting up on her own. Also consider a high chair that has wheels and adjusts in height so you can feed baby while you sit at the kitchen table. Another great choice is a high chair that you can pull up to a regular table by removing the tray. If space is an issue in your kitchen, check out the more booster-like seats that sit atop one of your regular kitchen chairs. They don't take up the large footprint of a standalone high chair and they have many of the features of a full-size high chair.

Where to Put It

❏ Start by grouping like things together. For instance, if you're a coffee drinker, set up a coffee station near the coffee pot where you keep coffee mugs, creamer, sugar bowl, and spoon. Further, keep it simple, putting the coffee pot next to the sink and, if possible, using the sprayer to fill the pot with water.

❏ Following is a list of the main kitchen zones and what you need in those zones. Other zones to consider besides the ones mentioned include a beverage/snack station, bill-paying zone, and a Family Communications Center (see Chapter 15, General Home Organization).

Food Preparation Zone

Locate near: Sink, if possible

Items stored: Mixing bowls, measuring cups, wooden spoons, knives, cutting board, and miscellaneous appliances (mixer, chopper, blender)

Tip: Keep your knives sharpened, which always makes food prep easier. Also, keep a good-quality cutting board close by.

Cooking/Baking Zone

Locate near: Stove

Items stored: Spices, pots and pans, and utensils

Tip: Maintain the freshness of your baking supplies and avoid pesky critters by placing flour, sugar, and so on in sealed, labeled containers.

Serving Zone

Locate near: Kitchen table or eating area

Items stored: Serving dishes, plates, bowls, glassware, utensils, and napkins

Tips: If you're low on cabinet space but have room near the kitchen table, consider adding a sideboard or buffet to house dishes, plates, and bowls. That makes for easy access when setting the table for a meal. If you tend to plate food at the counter area, locate plates, dishes, and bowls in a cabinet close to the stove.

Cleaning/Dishwashing Zone

Locate near: Sink/dishwasher

Items stored: Soap, sponges

Tips: If possible, store cleaning supplies in an overhead cabinet to avoid little ones gaining access. To avoid dishpan hands, wear rubber gloves when cleaning pots and pans. Keep hand lotion nearby.

Food Storage Zone

Locate near: Refrigerator

Items stored: Tupperware or GladWare containers for leftovers, along with plastic wrap and tinfoil.

 good idea!
Dedicate a particular area in the refrigerator for the leftovers so they don't get pushed to the back and become a science experiment gone bad. Incorporate leftovers into upcoming meals.

Baby Zone

Locate near: Inside the pantry or designate a cabinet and/or shelf near the sink/dishwasher

Items stored: Containers for bottles, nipples, sippy cups, pacifiers, formula, baby food, bibs, baby utensils, and any other kitchen-related baby items you may have

Tips:

- Group these items together on one shelf or in one cabinet. You may need to create the space by shifting current items, but do make the effort so you don't wind up with a countertop full of baby items.

- Divide the space within the cabinet or pantry, keeping the food separate from the bottle and Binky paraphernalia. Include a container for bibs and one for child-size utensils, baby spoons, plates, and cups.

Group like items together on pantry shelves.

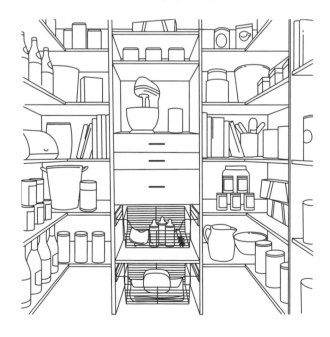

- As your baby grows and you transition from bottles to sippy cups, store cups assembled (they usually come with three parts—the cup base, the top, and a "stopper") so when you need one, you know all the parts are accounted for.
- If you're not in a position to install semi-custom or custom pullout drawers to make low cabinets easier to access, use baskets that can easily be pulled out to contain items, such as pot lids, sippy cups, and other small items. Use one basket per category.

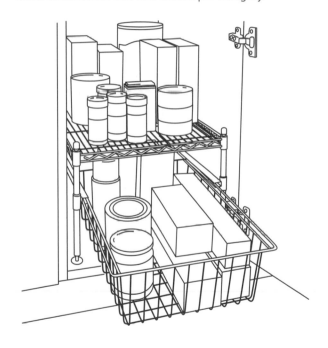

Pull-out drawers help make low cabinet spaces accessible.

 good idea!
Always leave at least one clean bib hanging on the high chair or lying on the tray so when it comes time to feed baby, you're ready!

Tips for Organizing and Maintaining Your Kitchen

Here are some general tips for keeping the kitchen—often the most-used room of the house—operating in a smooth, orderly fashion.

- **Place items where you use them**—For instance, put the pots and pans in the lower cabinets closest to the stove, and place the spices in the upper cabinets directly next to the stove or nearby.

- **Eliminate duplicates**—If you have more than one set of everyday dishes, consider rotating them with the seasons to unclutter your cabinet space. Put the extra sets out of the way, perhaps in your attic.

- **Use a lazy Susan to double cabinet space**—This spinner works great for spices or canned goods. Pull-down spice racks also work well—they keep spices in place and allow you to take advantage of vertical shelf space.

- **Be sure your glassware set is intact**—Throw away chipped glasses. For a family of four, have at least eight to ten glasses, perhaps of different sizes.

- **Clean out your refrigerator and freezer on a regular basis.** Performing this task prior to going food shopping is a great way to see what you really need and will ensure leftovers that have been pushed to the back are not forgotten. Zone the refrigerator and designate a particular shelf for leftovers; place condiments in the door shelves; butter, margarine, and sour cream on another shelf; and so on. Group like items together.

- **Organize to make hosting easier.** Having an organized kitchen will also allow guests and visitors to locate what they need. If you're seated with baby in your arms and want to offer the guest a cup of coffee, for example, you can easily tell her where to get it without getting up from your seat.

- **When you organize a space, always leave room to grow** (as a rule of thumb, 20 to 25 percent).

- **Plan to run baby toys through the dishwasher from time to time, especially the ones that baby puts in her mouth** (teething rings are a good example). Consider buying a dishwasher basket for pacifiers, bottle nipples, and small items that could potentially float around the dishwasher. These baskets come in very handy!

countertops are not for storage

Countertops are valuable real estate in the kitchen meant to be used as a workspace where you prepare food and keep appliances you use regularly (for example, a coffee pot or a toaster). If you're using the countertops to house items that don't fit into those categories, consider purging items in the cabinets to make room or relocating nonkitchen items to another part of the house. For example, put paperwork in the office or projects in closed storage in the family room.

Meal Planning

Mealtimes generally happen in one of two ways once baby has arrived:

1. Baby cooperates fully while you prepare dinner, then as soon as you sit down, he begins fussing and you're unable to eat peacefully.
2. Preparing dinner is a major challenge because he's fussy, but then you are able to sit and eat, perhaps while giving baby a bottle or putting him in a bouncy seat.

Either way, it can be a challenge to get through mealtime after baby arrives because you're either tired by that time of day or baby requires attention, and it can be challenging to perform both the roles of mommy and cook. If you're fortunate to have a baby who settles down for the night around 7:00 P.M., you may want to consider a quiet dinner at that time.

Consult your recipe books for recipe ideas, but remember to keep it simple when baby is new so you're able to easily complete the task of preparing a meal while caring for baby. Check out Appendix B for some great books and websites to help with meal planning.

What You Need
❑ Complete the Meal Planner form (see page 243) prior to writing out your grocery list. Make a master grocery list based on what you've planned to cook.

Where to Put It
❑ Put the Meal Planner form and the grocery list in the kitchen near your cookbooks. Consider keeping a coupon holder in this section, too.

Mealtime Tips

Here are some ideas to help you get through mealtime:

- **Feed baby while you eat (if bottlefeeding)**—Wait to feed baby until you sit down. Put baby in the infant carrier or reclining high chair; hold the bottle with one hand and eat with the other. Make sure you've cut your food prior to giving baby the bottle or it will not be possible to accomplish these two tasks at once.

- **Plan to eat after baby is down for the night**—If your baby goes to bed as early as 7:00 P.M. or 7:30 P.M., it may make sense to wait to eat dinner at that time when you and your partner can reconnect and have an uninterrupted conversation. You'll want to incorporate baby into the mealtime process once she is sitting up and begins eating solids.

- **Keep your expectations low**—There will be times when you can make a meal from start to finish with baby's cooperation. Perhaps he's sitting happily in a bouncy seat or lying on the floor playing, but typically, at some point, baby gets fussy and you will wind up not able to sit down and eat the meal you've prepared. If you are able to sit down with your partner for a meal without having to get up numerous times to attend to baby, consider that an amazing feat.

- **Plan a menu for the week**—Prepare a few meals in advance, then freeze them. Initially, plan on eating those types of easy-to-prepare meals until you're in a routine with baby. Stock up the freezer with frozen pizzas or make big batches of chili or spaghetti sauce to freeze in portion-sized containers. There's no need to sacrifice nutrition. There are lots of cookbooks on the market today that provide recipes and techniques for cooking a nutritious, quick meal. See Appendix B for recommendations.

06 Organizing the Bathroom

This chapter provides step-by-step guidance on what you need and where to put it, including what to keep on hand and what to store elsewhere if space is limited. The chapter includes how to set up specific "baby" areas for towels, shampoos, bath toys, and more.

> **Problem—Solved!**
>
> Amy didn't know where to begin when organizing her bathroom. Among other items, she struggled with what to do with the overwhelming number of travel-sized bottles she had accumulated, how to sort her makeup and toiletry items, and where to place the extra rolls of toilet paper and cleaning supplies. Now with a baby on the way, she had to find *more* space for the slew of baby items she needed on hand in the bathroom. She utilized the GOPACK method to eliminate excess, assign homes for the items that would live in the space, and plan how to contain the items.

Look at What You Have

If you're lucky enough to have one bathroom dedicated to baby, organization may be less challenging. However, if the bathroom is shared, you'll want to be precise with the zoning to fit all the necessary supplies.

Nowadays, it's uncommon for medicine cabinets to be a standard item installed in newer construction—plain mirrors are generally what you'll find. If you don't have a medicine cabinet, consider installing one to hold toothpaste/toothbrush, nail polish, prescriptions, cosmetics, contact lens solution, razors and shaving lotion—the items that need to be up and out of reach of little ones, but accessible for daily use. Medicine cabinets usually come with adjustable shelving, so group items by height if possible and then arrange your shelves accordingly. In the shower area, use a shower caddy that hangs from the shower head to organize shampoo, conditioner, loofah, and so on. These two solutions alone will help contain items that might otherwise sit on the vanity tops and in the shower, making it more difficult to quickly clean surfaces.

*An organized
medicine cabinet.*

Baby's Bathroom Items

Though you may not need to bathe your newborn every single day, you still need quite a few items on hand.

What You Need

- ❑ Portable tub
- ❑ Bath ring (once baby is sitting up)
- ❑ Washcloths
- ❑ Towel—hooded towels work well (have a couple of extra on hand)
- ❑ Baby shampoo/soap
- ❑ Pitcher or cup to add water to bathe or rinse baby (when you rinse baby's head, cover her forehead with a washcloth)
- ❑ Bath toys
- ❑ Wastepaper basket
- ❑ Hamper* (if not in the bathroom, make sure there's one in the nursery)
- ❑ Knee pad* (use a gardening kneepad while you bathe baby)
- ❑ Cleaning caddy (with surface cleaners and paper towels or sponges for easy bathroom cleanup—store it under the sink)

* Nice, but not necessary.

Where to Put It

- ❑ Keep the linens in the linen closet in or adjacent to the bathroom (if you have one) or in the baby's nursery.
- ❑ Make space in the bathroom, perhaps under the sink, to house your kneepad, pitcher or other container for rinsing baby, and baby shampoo and soap. If your under-the-sink cabinet is stocked with extra toilet paper and cosmetics, consider relocating those items to the linen closet (or storage closet) and medicine cabinet.

❏ Hang the bath toys in the tub area using a great product called the Frog Pod Bath Toy Drain and Storage by Boon, or something comparable, which makes for easy cleanup and storage because you can scoop up and rinse off bath toys and hang them up to store and dry.

Your Bathroom

If you have your own master bathroom, you may find that it needs organizing as well. Clutter forms in many areas of the bathroom: under the sink, on the vanity, on the back of the toilet, and in the shower. Here are some suggestions for reducing the clutter in your bathroom:

- Downsize on the cosmetics—choose and use only your favorites.
- Remove outdated prescriptions, vitamins, lotions, and so on. You'll be surprised at the number of expired prescriptions you may have on hand.
- Pack a travel bag and a guest bag full of sample sizes and donate the rest to a nearby homeless shelter. How many do you *really* need?
- Use the vanity top only for soap, a hand towel, and perhaps a glass or toothbrush holder (you could also hang a toothbrush holder on the wall or put the toothbrushes in the vanity).
- Use drawer space for small items such as cosmetics and under-the-sink space for tall bottles and extra toilet paper. If space allows, use a lazy Susan under the sink for ease of access and storage of tall containers or a double-stacking lazy Susan to further maximize space.

Purging

Items to be purged include expired medication and shampoos you don't use (consider a basket of guest supplies for these and travel-sized items). You can also discard these items after the following time periods:

Bar soap:
18 months to 3 years
Bath gel, body wash:
3 years
Bath oil:
1 year
Body lotion:
3 years
Conditioner:
2 to 3 years
Deodorant, opened:
1 to 2 years
Deodorant, unopened:
2 years
Eye cream, opened:
1 year
Eye cream, unopened:
3 years
Face lotion:
3 years
Foundation, oil-based:
2 years
Foundation, water-based:
3 years
Hair gel:
2 to 3 years
Hairspray:
2 to 3 years

Lip balm, opened:
1 year
Lip balm, unopened:
5 years
Lipstick:
2 years
Mascara, opened:
3 to 4 months
Mascara, unopened:
2 years
Moist wipes:
2 years
Mouthwash:
3 years from the manufacturer's date
Nail polish:
1 year
Perfume:
1 to 2 years
Rubbing alcohol:
3 years
Shampoo:
2 to 3 years
Shaving cream:
2 years plus
Tooth-whitening strips:
1 year

07 | Organizing the Master Bedroom

The master bedroom should truly be a retreat and sanctuary. It's an escape from the daily demands of life and a place to re-energize. This chapter exists to assist moms- and dads-to-be in creating a balance between hosting your newborn at certain times and easily transforming your space into a couples' retreat. Prior to adding baby paraphernalia in the space, we'll look at how to effectively use your space for *you*! Later, we'll deal with adding the baby items.

Problem—Solved!

Jane and Austin needed a quiet place to rest at the end of the day. Jane worked from home and found that in order to unwind and get a restful night's sleep after putting the baby down in his nursery, it was important for her to have a soothing environment. The couple opted to eliminate their television and instead added a CD player to enjoy music and audiobooks from time to time. They also splurged on some luxurious bedding that they found at a discount store. Their room provided a great space to end the day. When they needed to get up in the middle of the night to check on their son it didn't seem to be a horrible interruption because they had given themselves the opportunity to unwind and relax.

Early on, the couple added a "baby zone" in the bedroom, which consisted of a Pack 'n Play for baby to sleep in for a while and a portable changing basket containing what they needed for nighttime changes.

What You Need

❑ Bed

❑ Chair*

❑ Dresser

❑ Nightstands, preferably with storage*

* Nice, but not necessary.

What You *Don't* Need

- **Computer**—Put this in the office or family room.

- **Exercise equipment**—Unless concealed behind a movable screen of some sort. You don't need a constant visual reminder of working out, especially if you're in a mode of not doing so.

- **Laundry to be folded**—Get it out of sight, even if it means putting it in a laundry basket in the closet until it's time to fold. Remember to make time to get it folded!

- **Television**—It's a personal decision whether or not you choose to put a TV in your bedroom. If you want a TV, consider a flat screen since they are less obtrusive. The key to remember is that TV can be a distraction from communication, and bedtime may be the only time of day you, as a couple, get some quiet time to talk.

Where to Put It

❑ If you haven't already made your master bedroom into a retreat, consider using the Space Planning 101 guidelines in Chapter 4 to evaluate the space, determine a focal point, and then zone the space. Then you can put items in their appropriate zones.

Zones in the Master Bedroom

The zones in the master bedroom include:

- **Sleeping Zone:** This is where the bed lives. You may want to consider under-the-bed storage for extra blankets and sheets, utilizing a roll-out container for those items. Avoid storing miscellaneous items under the bed so you are actively using the space.

- **Reading Zone:** Consider a comfortable reading chair and table to hold a lamp, your books, and a beverage. If you don't have this option, due to space or choice, use the bedside table to hold your books/magazines, eyeglasses (if needed), and other items such as hand/body lotion, a nail file, lip balm, and paper and pencil, preferably in closed storage. Do your best to eliminate the visual clutter of these areas—it'll look nicer and it's easier to clean.

- **Entertainment Zone:** This zone includes the electronics you choose to have in your bedroom (if any)—television, DVDs, remote controls, and music players. If you have a flat-screen TV, you may opt to hang it on the wall over the dresser, perhaps. If so, eliminate the clutter by using one of the dresser drawers for the DVDs, remote controls, and so on, so the top of the dresser doesn't become a storage area for these items. You can keep a minimal supply of DVDs here and put the rest with your collection in the main living space.

- **Dressing Zone:** The dressing zone is where your clothes live and where you primp yourself for the day. This area may include your closet and the vanity area in the bathroom. This zone may technically extend beyond the bedroom itself depending upon your home's setup. If you don't have a walk-in closet, try to develop a routine of placing your clothing in a particular place for when you get dressed. Men's valets work well. If you're a working mom, choose clothes the night before—it saves time in the morning, especially if you need to iron something. You can hang your clothes on the doorknob of the closet (or on an over-the-door hook that doesn't require installation) for the next day as long as the hangers are put back in the closet. The items kept in the closet area include clothing and accessories, and perhaps jewelry. If at all possible, keep these items together. If you find that there's a tremendous overflow, reassess the space to see if you could better organize the closet area (see Chapter 8 on closet organization for tips and strategies for maximizing the closet space). In your vanity area, minimize the number of cosmetics and choose favorites. Eliminate the rest. You know, those "just in case" items that have been lurking around for years. See Chapter 6, Organizing the Bathroom.

The Baby Zone Within the Master Bedroom

Initially, baby will probably sleep in your room. It's great to have him nearby for middle-of-the-night feeding and changing.

Problem—Solved!

Jan and Eric had always enjoyed their master bedroom. After they were married, they made it a priority to create a sanctuary to retreat to at the end of the day. With a new baby arriving, a friend suggested that they put a bassinet in their bedroom so that Jan could recover from the delivery and not have to trek to the nursery each time the baby needed attention, and so they could easily share night-time feedings (since they chose to bottle-feed). Since the couple's goal was to eventually have the baby sleep through the night in her nursery, they made a conscious decision to set up a temporary baby zone in their room to house any necessities.

What You Need for a Baby Zone in Your Bedroom

❑ Bassinet/Pack 'n Play

❑ Bottle warmer*

❑ Portable changing basket or container that houses diapers, wipes, and extra pajamas in the event baby's diaper leaks

❑ Nursing pillow to prop baby up while feeding

* Nice, but not necessary.

Where to Put It

❑ Consider dedicating a drawer in the nightstand to any baby-related items. Make sure these are frequently used items—you don't want the drawer to become a bottomless pit of baby items that accumulate in your room. If those items accumulate, make a habit of returning them to the nursery on a regular basis.

❑ Another option for temporarily storing baby items in the master bedroom is a hanging container in the closet for extra diapers, wipes, Onesies, and so on so you don't have to trek to the nursery. This works especially well if you live in a home where the master bedroom is on one floor and the nursery is on another.

Keep in mind: A baby zone in your master bedroom is a temporary solution. Ultimately, you will want to settle baby into her own space—the nursery—and use that space for her things. Maintain your retreat—your master bedroom—for a getaway once baby has been put down for the night so you can re-energize and relax in preparation for the next day.

08 | Organizing Closets

Have you ever walked into someone's house and it appears to be spotless, then you open a closet door and you discover where all the stuff is? We all have our secrets. Since this book is about organizing and helping you simplify so you can spend more time with your newborn, this chapter will help you sort out the master, linen, hall, guest room (if you've got one), and utility closets. We've already covered how to organize the baby's closet in Chapter 4, so now we'll focus on other areas.

Before You Start

Before diving into the task of organizing your closets, it's important to make a few considerations so that you get the results you want. The major consideration is to determine what will live in each closet—not what *currently* lives in the closets, but what *will* live in the closets. All too often, due to a shortage of closet space or lack of time spent on considering why something is being placed in a certain closet, they become filled with unrelated items. The goal is to simplify, so let's begin with a plan.

First, what you would like to see in each closet? This is important. Why? Once you've determined what will live in the closet, then you can zone the closet to ensure enough space for each category and that you will install the proper shelving, rods, drawer units, and so on to accommodate all that will be placed inside.

Here are examples of what items typically live in particular closets:

- **Master closet**—Clothing, shoes, bags, belts, accessories, laundry basket/sorter, and bag for dry cleaning.
- **Linen closet**—Sheets; towels; extra comforters, blankets, and pillows; extra toiletries. Consider space for a first-aid kit, prescriptions, and other medicines. Contain loose items in labeled bins for easy identification and access. Remember to place medicines up high so little ones can't get to them.
- **Hall closet**—Coats, jackets, accessories (gloves, hats, and so forth), shoes and boots, and tote bags. Consider a space for frequently used sporting items (for example, a basketball or a set of golf clubs). Leave room for guests to hang their coats when they visit. Add extra hangers for visitors' coats. This closet may also be used to house gift wrap (contained in a holder for easy access and use).
- **Utility closet**—Batteries, light bulbs, extra paper towels, cleaning supplies, tools, and electrical/computer wires.
- **Guest room closet**—This closet is great for housing gift wrap, gifts to give, luggage, memorabilia, and hobby or craft supplies. Since a guest room is generally not used on a daily basis, you could even use this space for crafting by setting up a portable table that can later be stored in the closet along with the supplies. Remember to leave hanging space (and extra hangers) for guests.

Take an Inventory

Make a list of the items that live in each closet and add a column to the list to show where those items *will* live when you're done organizing. (See page 225 for the Closet Inventory form.) This will also help you determine the best place to keep items. For example, you may keep the vacuum cleaner in the master closet due to lack of space, but once the utility closet is effectively zoned, you can make a space for it there.

How to Zone a Closet

Now it's time to assign zones to each closet. Sketch a picture of the closet, marking sections for each of the categories. Use your Inventory List to check off each item to make sure you've accounted for everything.

Example layout of a guest room closet.

Storage Options for Closets

Here are some items that I recommended for closet organization:

- Containers—baskets, clear plastic boxes with tops, hat boxes, tall trash can–style containers for gift wrap rolls.
- Rods/shelving
- Hangers

Remember to label all containers!

Maximizing Space in Closets

Try these ideas to make the most of the space you have:

- Use the walls to hang belts and scarves.
- Store sweaters in clear containers on top shelves.
- Maximize the vertical space of the closet and install shelving up top for out-of-season clothing. If the vertical space is easily reachable, consider containers to hold purses.
- Double your closet hanging space by adding a vertical rod extender that hangs down from the upper rod, allowing you to short-hang clothing above and on the rod below. These are available at most large retailers and home improvement stores. Generally, you don't even need any tools to install them.
- Utilize shoe racks on the floor to contain shoes.

Organizing Your Master Closet

These tips will help you organize a master closet before you have maternity clothes to deal with.

GOPACK Your Closet

Before your tummy begins to expand is a great time to get your closet organized. Begin by storing out-of-season clothing and eliminating clothing that hasn't been worn in at least one year. Next, follow these simple steps:

1. Clear your bed or floor space so you have room to work.
2. Begin by grouping like pieces together: shirts, pants, suits, dresses, and so on.

3. Go through each pile and separate the clothing into one of the following categories:
   - **Keep**—These items will return to the closet.
   - **Donate**—Give these pieces to a charity. Make sure they're still wearable (no stains or missing buttons).
   - **Consign**—This pile will go to a consignment store. Check your local store's guidelines for consigning.
   - **Give away**—These items go to friends or family members.
4. Zone your closet. Choose specific areas for each category of clothing/shoes/purses. By placing like items together, you'll gain a clear perspective on what you actually own and be able to find things when you want them.
5. Put like items together and contain when possible. For example, you can store handbags on a top shelf in clear, labeled containers.
6. Separate the keep pile into colors (within each type of clothing). This gives you a good perspective on how many black T-shirts you own and whether or not you really need to keep all of them.
7. Put everything in its appropriate place.

Tips for Letting Go of Clothing

Many women have difficulty parting with clothing. These ideas may help you make decisions:

- If you haven't worn it during the season, say goodbye.
- If you don't like the way you feel when you're wearing a piece of clothing, get rid of it.
- Make space for what you love!
- If you're struggling with not fitting into pre-pregnancy clothing (which is normal and okay), consider storing the pre-pregnancy clothes to remove the daily reminder of where you used to be. When

A master closet with vertical and horizontal space utilized.

you're a new mom, it's important to remind yourself of what a great job you're doing and a visual reminder of your pre-pregnancy body can be a bit of a downer. If having the clothing in your closet is a motivator, by all means, keep it hanging.

The Ins and Outs of Maternity Clothing

Once you know you're pregnant, you'll need to zone a specific area in your closet just for maternity clothing. Most likely you will have fewer pieces of maternity clothing than your usual wardrobe, so you won't need a ton of space. Assigning a specific area just for maternity will also help you easily weed them out once they're no longer needed. Again, separate by shirts, pants, skirts, and so on.

You'll be able to wear some of your regular clothing in the first trimester and again as you transition from maternity to regular clothing. However, the fact is that many of us don't get back into our pre-pregnancy clothing right away, if at all. It takes time. So you may need your pregnancy clothes longer than you think. Luckily, you can maintain your existing style while you're pregnant. It's important to feel comfortable in your clothing while pregnant because your body will go through many changes. Clothing manufacturers now offer modern and stylish maternity clothing for moms-to-be in virtually every price range. What a relief!

 good idea!

Most of us would love to fantasize that our belly will immediately shrink back to its pre-pregnancy size and shape, but let's get real. Don't expect to get back into those smaller-size jeans you were wearing pre-pregnancy for at least a little while. To some extent, the belly naturally reduces in size, but you may need to work off the final inches with your exercise of choice. With your doctor's approval, you can begin by simply walking your baby around the block in her stroller!

Transitional and Nursing Clothing

Transitional clothing is a great way to ease into or out of your pregnancy clothes. Some transitional clothing is also nursing-friendly. Lots and lots of choices exist today that will complement your personal style and provide comfort too. The typical pregnant woman begins to show at about four months. However, some women do show earlier. See Appendix B for companies offering transition clothing.

You may need to wear your pregnancy bottoms for a couple of months, but with products like the Bella Band, you may be able to get back into your pre-pregnancy pants and jeans sooner just like when you

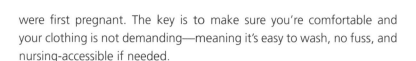

were first pregnant. The key is to make sure you're comfortable and your clothing is not demanding—meaning it's easy to wash, no fuss, and nursing-accessible if needed.

Buying

Along with the longtime maternity clothing retailers (such as Motherhood Maternity and A Pea in the Pod), stores such as Target, GAP, and Old Navy are also carrying maternity clothing. You can also find options online, including petite and plus-size maternity wear. If there's one near you, visit an independently owned maternity store and get to know the owner and sales staff. Establish a relationship and they will be happy to contact you when new items come in or when that top you love goes on sale.

Try the simple approach of buying mostly solids (rather than lots of prints) so you can mix and match. Even though by the end of your pregnancy it will feel like it's lasted forever, pregnancy is a relatively short period of time. Therefore, be clear on how much money you want to invest in maternity clothing and stick to your budget.

 good idea!
To avoid stretching out your pre-pregnancy underwear, purchase maternity panties. With the range of options available today, you can essentially duplicate the current style you wear in a maternity cut—including a thong!

Purchase some basic pieces and add others throughout your pregnancy. If your budget is slim, buy secondhand clothing or borrow from a friend. In reality, no one expects your pregnancy wardrobe to rival your existing wardrobe, but you can purchase some key pieces and still stay within a budget and remain true to your personal style.

Many moms struggle with how much to buy. A starter wardrobe of eight to nine pieces is a sensible way to go: a T-shirt, a flirty top, a versatile pullover, an everyday dress, a classic pair of shorts, a pair of go-anywhere pants, a flattering pair of jeans, and a short skirt. There's the tried-and-true Pregnancy Survival Kit by Belly Basics that offers a four-piece set, including a dress, pants, skirt, and a top. It's made of a cotton/Lycra material, so it's great for early in pregnancy, as well as transitioning after baby is born. There's both a winter and summer version of this kit. Accessories—shoes, bags, jewelry, and hair accessories—can spice up your wardrobe and should fit for your entire pregnancy and beyond. Here are some specific lists for moms-to-be.

What You Need

- ❏ Khaki, black, or neutral-colored pants—several pairs
- ❏ Jeans
- ❏ Comfy pair of pajamas—avoid your husband's boxers and T-shirt to maintain a feminine, sexy feel.
- ❏ Two pairs of comfortable shoes—remember, your feet may swell a bit while pregnant. If you're a high-heel–wearing woman, consider a lower, sturdier heel to maintain your balance. Adjusting to body and weight changes can be tricky, and you want to stay balanced.
- ❏ Bella Band—when your pre-pregnancy pants begin to get tight, you can continue to wear them unbuttoned but supported by the band.
- ❏ T-shirts—find a good fit and buy one in every color
- ❏ Empire-waist tops—a great choice for a pregnant woman
- ❏ Skirt
- ❏ Versatile dress that could be worn with a blazer or sweater, and shoes or boots.
- ❏ Maternity bathing suit and shorts, if you're in the season

What You Need: Additional Items for the Working Mom-to-Be

- ❑ At least one or possibly two suits that include a blazer, pants, and a skirt (black and a neutral color)
- ❑ A couple of dresses: one semi-formal to formal (black is always a good choice and by adding jewelry and a dressy bag you make it formal) and one casual
- ❑ White button-down shirt

Consignment

Local consignment shops may offer a maternity section, which is a great way to purchase gently used clothing at a reduced price. Check your local phone book or search Google.com for consignment shops in your area. Also try eBay.com or other online sources for gently worn maternity clothing, especially in a brand whose sizes you are familiar with. These outlets are also options for selling your maternity clothing once you've finished having babies.

Borrowing

If you choose to borrow from a friend, make sure you take good care of the clothing. Tell your friend that you appreciate her generosity and that you will return the clothing to her in the same condition. If you happen to wear out a piece of borrowed clothing or wind up with a stain that cannot be removed, replace the piece of clothing with something comparable to avoid being labeled a "bad borrower."

If you borrow from more than one friend, devise a way to distinguish which piece of clothing belongs to whom, which can be accomplished by putting a mark on the clothing label (for example, red for Mary Ann, black for Susie). But first ask the person you've borrowed from if this is the best way to handle the situation—she may not want marks on the labels of her clothing.

Also, ask the lender how she cares for her clothing. Some may wash and hang the clothing so it doesn't wear out as quickly. Others may wash and dry. It's best to ask questions like this in advance:

- Would you prefer I wash and hang the clothing?
- Would you prefer I dry clean the suits and dresses?
- When do you expect me to return the clothing (one week or one month after the baby arrives, or does it matter)?

Where to Put It: Zoning Your Master Closet

Draw a rough sketch of the closet and designate space for the items you are keeping. Remember to purge before you contain so you can effectively zone the closet space. Consider the following when organizing your master closet:

❑ Maximize your hanging space, both long and short. Try using a double-hanging rod extender and hanging closet organizers to expand vertical space.

❑ Use shelves for purses and folded clothing (T-shirts and workout clothing).

❑ Get a belt hanger (either attached to the wall or one that hangs on a rod).

❑ Use a hanging jewelry holder*—easy to see and access what you own.

❑ Add drawers* to the shelving unit to house socks and underwear if you don't have a dresser.

❑ Find space on upper shelves to store containers for out-of-season (or in this case, pre-pregnancy clothing) and rarely worn or used items.

* Nice, but not necessary.

Where to Put It: Zoning Your Master Closet—*continued*

❑ Bring in shoe racks on the floor. (Avoid placing shoes on shelves over clothing to avoid debris falling on your clothing.) Use clear containers with lids to hold shoes and stack them on shelves, or purchase shoe racks that sit on the floor. Hanging shoe organizers are a great way to keep shoes from getting kicked to the back of the closet, too. They can also be used to hold handbags or rolled up T-shirts.

❑ Laundry sorter, basket, or hamper

What You *Don't* Need in the Master Closet

• **Holiday decorations**—place these in the attic, under-the-stairs storage, or in the garage. These items are accessed once a year. Leave reachable storage space for items accessed more regularly.

• **Personal papers**—unless this is where you decide to stash your fireproof safety box that contains your important documents.

• **Sporting equipment**—store these in the garage or hall closet.

• **Photos**—store these in a guest or office closet.

• **Anything unrelated to what you wear**—remember to put things where you use them.

 good idea!

Simply, simplify, simplify! You'll be short on time when you have a new baby to take care of. Therefore, wash-and-wear clothing is essential—not only will you be able to get dressed and ready in a flash, you will also save cash on dry cleaning. Wear clothing that is comfortable and low maintenance—you don't want to have to pull out the ironing board. Also consider simplifying your hairstyle and makeup regimen, which will help you limit the amount of time it takes to get ready.

Organizing the Linen Closet

The linen closet has the potential to become a catchall for items that don't obviously belong in another place. If possible, utilize the linen closet strictly for linens and related items. Try to keep yours in good working order by following these tips:

- Store like items with like items. Create one shelf for sheets, one for towels, one for prescription and cosmetic items, and another for appliances. If possible, put a laundry basket on the floor of the linen closet to collect used towels. Label all shelves.

- For simplicity's sake, consider using all white linens, including towels. The benefit is that you can bleach all of the items to ensure they're really clean and you can wash them together, maximizing your washing/drying time.

- If you choose to use colored towels and linens, use one color for each family member, which will make it easier to keep track of which towel belongs to whom.

- You'll probably need three to four towels per person and two sets of sheets per person—that way when you remove the sheets you can immediately put another set on the bed.

What You Need

- ❑ Sheets/pillowcases
- ❑ Towels
- ❑ Spare toiletries and cosmetics (in labeled containers)
- ❑ Extra bedding (comforters, shams, and so on)
- ❑ Supplies: toilet paper, cleaning supplies, paper towels
- ❑ Medicines and prescriptions (stored in labeled containers for easy identification and access)

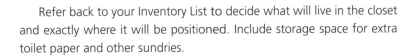

Refer back to your Inventory List to decide what will live in the closet and exactly where it will be positioned. Include storage space for extra toilet paper and other sundries.

Container Ideas for Linen Closets

Recommended containers:

- Clear, plastic boxes with tops that secure to keep items intact
- Milk-crate-type containers for heavier items
- Vertical shelf dividers to keep linens neatly stacked

Organizing the Hall Closet

Hall closet organization is critical to eliminating clutter in the entry area of your home. Therefore, it's important to save this closet for items that you and your family use regularly. For example, jackets, coats, shoes, storage for purse and briefcase, dog leash, and so forth.

Zoning the Hall Closet

Assign zones for:

- Jackets/coats, gloves/hats
- Shoes/boots
- Sporting equipment used on a regular basis (if possible, place these items in the garage, but if one is not available, make a space in the hall closet)
- Giftwrap and associated supplies (in a closed container)

Small pockets help contain various items.

Other Tips

Here are some other tips:

- Hang up jackets, then use the top shelf for a couple of baskets to hold gloves/mittens/scarves or goggles/hats/sunscreen for warm-weather months.

- Use cedar shoe shelving or hanging storage to house shoes that are most often worn (stick to just two pair per person to not overload this space with shoes—others can be stored in bedroom closets).

- Avoid placing "storage items" in this closet, unless you are making use of rarely accessed vertical space. If so, keep it to a minimum and label boxes that are stored on those shelves so you can easily identify what's up there.

- Consider using an over-the-door shoe holder for smaller items, including shoes, but leave room for items such as a flashlight, dog leash, keys, incoming and outgoing mail, coupon book, and other small items that are "active" that you need access to and that move regularly.

Organizing the Utility Closet

Utility closets are typically located in the laundry room or in a hallway near the kitchen. They are generally smaller in size, but a great place to keep items such as batteries, extension cords, cleaning supplies, glue, tape, and so on.

Again, group like items together, zone the space, and contain items. Be deliberate about what lives in this space. Add shelving where necessary to hold containers with various items (for example, separate attachments or extension cords). Leave enough vertical space if you're storing a vacuum cleaner and/or mops and brooms.

Other Tips

Here are more recommendations for organizing the utility closet:

- Install proper shelving to accommodate what will live in the closet
- Use clear plastic bins with lids (due to the heaviness of some items—batteries, for example—you'll want a durable container)
- Consider an over-the-door clear pocket container to house miscellaneous related items
- Utilize wall space in the closet to hang brooms and mops

Remember to label each container for easy identification and access.

09 | Organizing Your Home's Entryways

Everyone needs a space to put shoes, coats, stroller, diaper bag, and more. This chapter will help you organize the necessary items that you and your family frequently transport into and out of your home.

Entry Hall

If your front door is the main entry to your house, you'll want to set up a functional area for items that come and go when you do. Think of the front hall and its closet as a "container" for the personal belongings you take with you each day and bring home each evening. It's not a storage area, but more like a "launch pad"—a temporary place for items that come and go as you do. Do not leave items in the entry hall that you don't use on a daily basis. Use the hall closet mainly for coats/jackets, shoes, backpacks, stroller, and so on. In other words, not for permanently stored items such as photos, electronics boxes that you need to hold on to for the warranty period, and so on. Place those items in the garage, attic, or basement.

Organizing your entry hall can be easy because you're only dealing with a few items, many of which are small. You'll need a place for your keys, shoes, jackets, and bags (handbag, diaper bag, project bag, and so on).

What You Need

- ❑ Shoes
- ❑ Keys
- ❑ Purse/wallet
- ❑ Diaper bag/project bags/briefcase or work bag
- ❑ Stroller
- ❑ Mail—incoming and outgoing
- ❑ Electronics (iPod, MP3 player, cell phone)

Where to Put It

- ❑ Locker storage that can go up against a wall.
- ❑ If the space is limited, use your wall space! Hang hooks and install a shelf with baskets for smaller items. Use hooks for your everyday bags as well as others—for example, items to return to a store, a project bag, and a diaper bag.
- ❑ If you're without a hall closet, consider a coat rack and concealed or semi-concealed shoe storage that looks like a piece of furniture.
- ❑ It's great if you can fit a drawer unit to house smaller items so they are contained, but not visible.
- ❑ Place a key rack on the wall near the front door . . . and keep it up at your eye level so little ones can't get ahold of keys.
- ❑ Add hooks to the inside of the closet door at kid level so you can hang bags for your little one. Once he reaches about two or three years old, you can teach him to hold his own bag and put it away when you arrive home.

Mudroom

The mudroom is typically an entryway that is accessed through or near the garage and adjacent to the kitchen. The benefit of a mudroom is that what you store will not generally be seen by visitors (who probably enter through the front entrance of the home), which gives you a little more flexibility in terms of the type of storage you use. You can get away with more open containers versus the preferred concealed storage in the entryway so it doesn't look cluttered.

If you have both a mudroom and an entryway, evaluate how each space is used and when. Then zone and contain appropriate items in each space.

Each family member can claim his or her own cubby.

What You Need

❑ A place to put dirty shoes when you take them off

❑ Backpacks, umbrellas, and jackets

❑ Bags (projects, returns, dry cleaning)

❑ Baskets for electronics and cell phones (place near an outlet to recharge these items where they're stored)

❑ Family Communications Center (see Chapter 15, General Home Organization, for the complete system)

Where to Put It

❑ Hang lockers or cubbies along the wall and make them the focal point of the space. Give each family member his or her own locker or cubby.

❑ Hang bags, backpacks, and umbrellas in the lockers.

❑ Put electronics and other small items in baskets near outlets.

❑ If you choose to locate the Family Communications Center (see Chapter 15, General Home Organization) in the mudroom area, place it on the wall closest to the adjacent room, which is most likely the kitchen. This will allow you ease of access.

Launch Areas

A launch area, or launching pad, is generally a permanent place in the household—typically near the most commonly used door to the house—that houses temporary items. For example, a launching pad could be where all the incoming and outgoing items needed for that day are placed—what we talked about in the entry hall section on page 96.

Launch areas can be created in almost any room, however. This is a sort of "Go Home" area for items that belong in other rooms in the home, but somehow wound up in that particular space. You can use any type of container for launch area items. The key is to remember that they are temporary spots to house items and they *must* be cleared out regularly. Consider assigning family members responsibility for different launch area containers so they get cleared out regularly.

The car is another area that tends to hold transitional items that are either going into the house or need to be dropped off somewhere else—returned to a friend or the library, perhaps. Refer to page 110 for more on organizing your car.

Suggested Launch Areas

Here are some locations that might benefit from a container or two to help everyone return items to their proper home:

- **Bottom or top of staircases**—to transport items up and down (use a "stair basket")
- **Entryway or mudroom**—for items to be returned to a store, incoming/outgoing mail, forms for school activities (use one container for each category)
- **Garage**—donation items (use a large, clear, labeled container or a large, sturdy bag that can live on a hook attached to the garage wall)
- **Car**—baby items: favorite toys, bottles, blankets (use a container that can easily be filled up and brought inside to unload)
- **Kitchen**—basket for items that need to "go home" to other areas of the house. This basket allows you to easily contain the clutter that accumulates on countertops and the kitchen table. As with all the others, empty the basket regularly.

10 | Organizing the Garage

The garage is a multifunctional space these days. For some, it's used to park cars; for others, it stores various items; and for still other families it is where the man of the house hosts his friends and watches sporting events. Whether you're a gardener, a golfer, a car enthusiast, a parent with active children, a carpenter, or couch potato, you can find a solution that works for you. It all depends upon your budget. If your budget is small, simply add some inexpensive shelving and containers to organize everything. If you have a large budget, you can completely outfit the garage with the latest in garage organization fittings from companies such as Sears, Garagetek, or Garagenous Zones. Heck, you could even include a refrigerator, flat screen TV, and sofa! Go further and put down some flooring.

Problem—Solved!

After Rob and Amy were married, they bought a starter home with a two-car garage. They filled it with sporting equipment (they are avid snow skiers, cyclists, and surfers), gardening equipment, never-unpacked boxes from the move, and Amy's brother's stuff from college that was staying until he returned from an extended back-packing trip to Europe. With a baby on the way, Rob and Amy had a goal of reorganizing their garage so they could fit at least one of their vehicles and the baby paraphernalia they expected to have to store.

To eliminate items that were currently stored on the floor, they installed overhead storage for Amy's brother's items since these didn't need to be accessed for a long period of time. They also used the overhead storage for their ski equipment since they lived in a warm climate and didn't ski as much as they used to.

They spent a few hours sorting through the unopened boxes that had been in the garage since the move, donating much of it and finding places inside the house for Rob's yearbooks and Amy's books from graduate school. Amy and Rob also took advantage of the unused wall space to hang beach chairs and other beach-related items, created a zone for gardening equipment, including the lawn-mower and edger, and installed a store-bought pulley system to hang their bicycles.

The result: The garage was clear for a vehicle and they were able to carve out a baby zone for both the strollers (regular and jogger) where they could be easily accessed.

Safety First

The important thing to remember when you have small children is that the garage needs to be a safe place for everyone. All hazardous chemicals and harmful tools need to be out of reach and even placed in locked cabinets to avoid any mishaps. You can teach a toddler what's off limits, but it's better to be safe than sorry. Toddlers are curious and will most likely want to investigate what's contained in the garage—after all, they'll see brightly colored bottles, fascinating tools, and equipment they're not familiar with. If these items are locked up and concealed, toddlers may be inquisitive at first but they'll eventually give up and move on to what they can access. Place baby and toddler items in a safe area of the garage that contains only child-friendly items.

Prioritize Your Needs

When organizing the garage, you need to first decide on the function of the space. Identifying how the garage will be used will then help you to determine the zones you need.

For example, if it's a priority to park the cars in the garage and create a space for baby gear, then you can easily zone three usable spaces—one for each car and one for baby's things. More likely than not, unless you live in a townhouse or condo, you'll need a section for tools and gardening equipment too. Look at what you have and determine what you want—then you can move on to zoning the space.

Zones Are Key

As with any other space, think zones, zones, zones. Zoning is especially important in the garage because it's a large space that houses many distinct groups of items. Here are some common zones for a garage: gardening tools/equipment, sporting equipment, automotive, carpentry/workbench area (including associated nuts and bolts), outdoor clothing and shoes, overhead storage, and recycling.

Once you've determined the zones, map out on a piece of paper where the zones will reside. Place frequently used zones in accessible positions. For example, recycling bins are best placed near the entry door to the garage so you can easily drop items in the bins. Holiday decorations can be placed in overhead storage since they are accessed only once a year. Sporting equipment, on the other hand, may best be positioned near the garage doors so items can easily be loaded into your vehicle or grabbed and taken outside. If you're a part-time carpenter, consider a zone dedicated to housing equipment and tools related to that hobby. Another use for the garage could be a hobby zone where you set up a work table and stool, and attach hobby tools and containers to hold supplies to the wall above the work table. Use the information provided here and your imagination to come up with the ultimate plan for you. The zones you may want to consider are on the following pages.

I've listed the most common items people own on the following pages; your possessions might vary. That's fine; just list what you have and zone accordingly.

Automotive Zone

What You Need

- ❑ Extra tires
- ❑ Jumper cables
- ❑ Oil change materials
- ❑ Windshield wiper fluid

Where to Put It

- ❑ Shelving
- ❑ Containers with tops
- ❑ An overhead pulley system for extra tires

Carpentry Zone

What You Need

- ❑ Hardware
- ❑ Paint/stains
- ❑ Tools
- ❑ Vacuum*—This is a great addition to a garage that serves more than one function, especially if you're doing carpentry or wood-work. It's also a great way to keep your vehicle clean.

* Nice, but not necessary.

Where to Put It

- ❑ Workbench
- ❑ Closed, lockable storage for hazardous, sharp items
- ❑ Containers with lids to hold harmful chemicals and paints—put them on a *very* sturdy shelf installed up high

Baby Gear Zone

What You Need

❑ Hang as much of your baby equipment as you can: stroller/carriage, wagon, baby pool, outdoor sand play, ride-on toys, and more.

❑ Initially you'll only need a space for a stroller or carriage, but you'll soon acquire other items, seasonal and otherwise, that your little one will use. Therefore, when planning a baby zone, leave room to grow.

Where to Put It

❑ Hooks

❑ Shelving or containers that attach to a wall (for items like beach toys)

❑ Containers for toys that sit on the shelving

❑ The Cezanne rack from the Art of Storage to house all your baby equipment. Be sure to secure it to the wall as instructed.

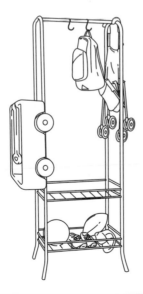

This rack can easily hold many large baby items.

Donation Zone

What You Need

❏ Any items that will be dropped off at a charity or picked up by one

Where to Put It

❏ In one bin (or more if necessary)

Gardening Zone

What You Need

❏ Place all associated items here: equipment to plant flowers and trim bushes, gardening gloves, potting soil, and so on.

Grouping like items together in the garage keeps it more functional.

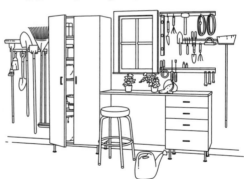

Where to Put It

❏ Closed, lockable storage for hazardous items (fertilizers, paints, chemicals)—place up high

❏ Gardening bench or work area if you pot flowers (You may want to consider a gardening bench outdoors to avoid dirtying the garage floor, unless you can easily clean it up.)

❏ Large, sturdy wall hooks or pulley system to hang tools or equipment (These can be purchased at large home improvement stores.)

Hobbies/Arts and Crafts Zone

What You Need

❑ If you have enough space, consider putting your arts and crafts materials in the garage.

❑ Stool or chair

Where to Put It

❑ Containers you can attach to the wall to hold small items

❑ Shelf attached to wall or bench

Recycling Zone

What You Need

❑ All of your home's recycling: glass, paper, plastic, newspapers, and so on

Where to Put It

❑ Large plastic containers—either a type your town or city gives you, or your own system personalized for your family's needs

❑ Mount a paper shredder over the paper recycling bin to dispose of private information safely.

Sports Zone

What You Need

- Balls (soccer, football, basketball, and so on)
- Bicycles
- Golf clubs
- Scooters
- Skateboards
- Ski equipment
- Sticks/bats

Where to Put It

- Bins for balls
- Pulley system to elevate bicycles (These may only be suitable for adult bicycles, but definitely use valuable overhead space.)
- Sports caddy to hold golf clubs, bats, shoes, and related items
- Wall hooks for ski equipment, scooters, and skateboards

All family members can easily find what they need with a caddy like this.

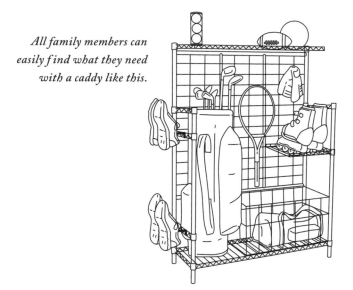

Where to Put Each Zone Within the Garage

❏ **Automotive:** Back wall of the garage.

❏ **Baby Gear:** On the wall in between the garage door and the entry door to the home.

❏ **Carpentry:** You'll likely need space to cut wood, paint items, and so on in this zone, so put the Carpentry zone in a section of the garage where you have room to spread out. For example, if you park your car on the right-hand side of the garage, consider placing the carpentry work area on the opposite side of the garage so there's plenty of room to work. Or, consider the back wall of the garage so you can possibly park a car, but still have access to this area. You'll also want to have electricity available to plug in power tools.

❏ **Donation:** Place near the entrance from the house into the garage, along with your Recycling zone. That way, you can easily gather, toss, and rid yourself of unwanted and unneeded items.

❏ **Gardening:** Place this zone closest to the garage door. You'll be doing your gardening outdoors, so you'll want to have all your supplies easily accessible to the exit.

❏ **Hobbies/Crafts:** Accessible location where you can fit a chair and have room to reach items you'll need. Consider placing near an electrical outlet if you're using items that require power, such as a glue gun.

❏ **Recycling:** Place near the entrance from the house into the garage. That way, you can easily toss items into the containers without having to walk too far into the garage, if at all. Include a Donations zone here too, to easily gather, toss, and rid yourself of unwanted and unneeded items.

❏ **Sports:** Generally, you should place this zone on the opposite side of the garage from the entrance into the home.

❑ **Work Supplies:** If you work from home or have your car packed with work supplies, designate a place in your garage to "park" those items when you're planning to use your car for social time. You might use a couple of shelves on a free-standing shelving unit. Only use this parking space for work-related items that you need to remove from your car—for example, a salesperson might need to transport samples and brochures; someone who runs a business putting on shows in people's homes (jewelry parties, kitchen supply parties, and so on) would need supplies for those events. That way, at a moment's notice, you can empty your work items and grab your beach bag.

Your Car(s)

For many of us, our car is a reflection of who we are. If you transport friends or clients in your car, you want to make sure that the reflection is a neat and clean one. When organizing your car, think in terms of zones: entertainment (CDs and DVDs), trash, beverages, and paper. Store items in appropriately sized containers. Case Logic (*www.caselogic.com*) manufactures a line of car accessories available through Target, K-mart, and other large retail stores.

Clear out your car on a regular basis: Take five minutes and empty the trash; remove empty cups and cans; and bring baby items, papers, and other paraphernalia into the house. This will save you from having to make several trips to and from the car to gather up items that are floating around.

What You Need

- ❏ Trash can/bag
- ❏ DVD/CD holder
- ❏ Dashboard-mounted holder for an MP3 player
- ❏ Container to transport items to and from car
- ❏ Trunk organizer(s): to hold groceries, extra outfit for baby and an extra shirt for you in the event yours gets stained while out and about. You could consider a standalone bag with pockets, a mesh bag, or one of the other options available.

Where to Put It

- ❏ **Trash can or bag:** Within reach of the driver's seat, perhaps hanging from the headrest of the passenger seat
- ❏ **CD holder:** Visor or glove box—within easy reach
- ❏ **Dashboard MP3 holder:** Within reach, wherever it fits best for driver
- ❏ **Container to transport items to and from car:** Trunk or back of SUV or station wagon
- ❏ **Trunk accessories:** Trunk area or back of SUV or station wagon

How to Organize Your Garage

Approach a garage organizing project as you would any other room of your house—fill out a Map form (see page 238) then follow the GOPACK method (visit Chapter 3 for a refresher course). Plan to spend a full day working on your garage. Although I recommend working for shorter times in other areas of your house, the garage is probably a bigger mess than all of those areas combined. In fact, it may well take you more than a full day; you may want to consider a full weekend (for example, six to seven hours one day and six to seven hours the next). Believe me, it'll be worth every moment when your garage is clean and usable!

Here are the steps to follow:

1. Try combining the Group and Purge steps of the process. Remove all items from the garage using tarps on the lawn or driveway to temporarily house items. As you remove items from the garage, make a decision about whether it will stay or go. Put items that are going in one pile, subdividing that pile into Consign or Donate sections (to family and friends or to a charity). Items you plan to keep should be grouped together on a separate tarp, sub-grouped with other like items (for example, tools with tools, sporting equipment with sporting equipment, and so on).

2. Sweep out and clean the garage floor and walls. Paint, if you choose to do so.

3. Zone the garage.

4. Install shelving, hooks, containers, and so forth.

5. Move items into their new home.

Tips for Effective Garage Organization

- Use labeled containers and closed storage to avoid items becoming soiled or winding up in a big heap.

- Use overhead and vertical storage, when possible. It's a great place to store holiday decorations or other items not accessed on a regular basis. Consider shelving such as Safe Racks to maximize the vertical storage.

- Do you ever wish you could simply and easily wash the garage floor of all its accumulated dust and debris? Consider a garage system or shelving that attaches to the walls and elevates all storage off the floor, which will enable you to easily spray the floor with a hose to clean it off.

- Place hooks near the door that leads from the garage to the interior of your home. Use these hooks for umbrellas and tote bags—frequently used items that need a home.

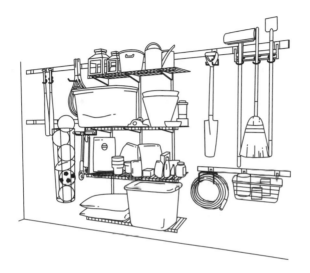

A wall-mounted storage system for the garage.

- Secure all free-standing shelving to the wall to ensure it can't be pulled over if a little one attempts to climb it.
- Use overhead storage to house lawn furniture if you live in a climate where you need to bring these items indoors during the winter months.

11 | Organizing the Office

Organizing an office space is critical in maintaining your sanity when it comes to paperwork. I once saw a diaper commercial that best visually illustrated the reality of having a baby: A new mom is sitting on her bed holding her newborn, the breeze is coming through the window, the curtains are flowing in the air, soft music is playing, and all appears to be peaceful. Then, suddenly, the next scene shows a flurry of activity in the front yard, toys all over, and a child is running around in a diaper. This is the reality of how fast things change! Before this reality sets in, let's get your office and paperwork organized so you can have peace of mind. From bills to the important papers you refer to every day to the paperwork that simply needs a home until it's time to retrieve it—setting up systems for your paperwork will keep your countertops clear and your bulletin board from being cluttered so you'll have easy access to the information you need.

Simple System for Baby Paperwork

Once you find out you're pregnant, you begin to gather information on pregnancy and nutrition, advice from other moms, dates of birthing classes, and much more. You could probably dedicate an entire drawer in a filing cabinet just to these kinds of documents! The key is to set up a simple system to track baby-related information so that you're organized and not overwhelmed. Consider using a portable container to hold Pendaflex files. It's nice to use a portable file so you can maintain control over the amount of paperwork and take it with you, say to sort and file while watching TV.

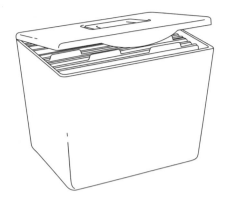

Portable file container.

Label the files with the following categories:

- Choosing a Pediatrician (use the "Choosing a Pediatrician" form at the back of this book)
- Birthing Classes/Education
- Nutrition
- Birth Certificate and Social Security Card
- Insurance Paperwork
- Immunizations and Vaccinations
- Thank-You Note Tracker and Gift Registry (use the Gift Tracker form on page 229)
- Pediatrician Visits and Healthcare Receipts
- Childcare Search (use the "Choosing a Childcare Provider" form on page 216)
- Save room for other categories that may emerge

Organizing the Office

Your office is probably a place that is prone to gathering piles of paper-work and items that don't belong there. Here's what you really need there and where to put it all.

What You Need:

- ❑ Desk
- ❑ Desk chair
- ❑ Other chair*
- ❑ Office supplies
- ❑ Computer/printer (and backup system: USB storage drive or external hard drive)
- ❑ Filing cabinet (which will use the Action/Reference system, explained on page 119)
- ❑ Desk lamp or sufficient overhead lighting

* Nice, but not necessary.

Where to Put It

- ❑ **Main work/desk area zone:** computer, desk chair, and desk lamp
- ❑ **Filing zone:** file cabinet(s)
- ❑ **Computing zone:** computer and printer, if not in work/desk zone
- ❑ **Reading zone:** a comfortable chair, table, and reading light
- ❑ **Office supplies/Storage zone:** Many people attempt to place ALL the office supplies they have on hand in one location; usually near the desk. Put one of each (for example, sticky notes, stapler, tape, etc.) in your desk and store the *extra* supplies in a closet or on a shelf in the space.

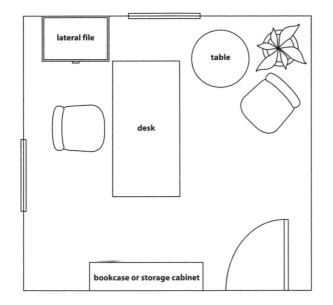

A possible office floor plan

Main Work/Desk Zone

For optimum comfort, place the desk so you are facing the door when seated in your desk chair. Use an ergonomically correct piece of furniture, if possible, with a keyboard drawer that is ergonomically correct. On your desk, you'll want to have a place for your telephone, pens, calendar, and paper.

The file drawer in a desk is best used for Active files. For example, current projects, your to-do list and the backup for the items on that list, files that you use on a daily basis, and ongoing paperwork that you need to access. All other paper should be filed in a Reference filing cabinet, which we'll get to in a moment. Always give yourself a clear space on the desk to open your calendar or spread out your papers in order to work. Oftentimes, desks become so cluttered that there's no actual work space.

Filing

Use a cabinet that houses Reference papers, which are documents that you need to have on file but which don't require any action on your part. Product manuals, paid bills, medical forms and insurance receipts, paid taxes, and car maintenance records are all examples of Reference papers. These are items that you can put your hands on if necessary but don't need to be in your desk drawer, which is reserved for active items.

Computing Zone

Your computer is probably in your main Work/Desk Zone, but if it's not, you'll need a separate place for it. Even if it is, you can consider it its own mini-zone since it requires a good amount of equipment and space. If you are using a model with a CPU and monitor, try to find a spot other than on top of your desk to place the CPU (such as under the desk or right next to it). If you haven't already, consider upgrading to a flat-screen monitor, which takes up dramatically less space. A laptop, of course, will provide you with the ability to easily move to another area which, when you have a baby, can be a good thing. For example, if the baby is in the bouncy seat in the family room and you want to check your e-mail, you can easily grab your laptop, sit on the couch or floor, and be right there with baby (of course, you need a wireless connection for this, which is also a worthwhile investment that provides flexibility and ease of movement).

Again, whenever possible, use ergonomically correct equipment. Install a keyboard drawer positioned so your hands are positioned below your elbows. If you are using a laptop yet want to maintain an ergonomically correct keyboard position for your desk space, consider a wireless keyboard and mouse.

Reading

If you choose to have a reading area in your office, choose a comfortable chair, a small end table to place a beverage, and proper lighting. This zone also does double-duty if you're working at your desk and your spouse/partner wants to join you for a conversation.

Office Supplies/Storage

This is the zone for shelving, containers for small items, and possibly a bookcase. You can use closet storage for all items or place some on a bookshelf, containing smaller items such as sticky notes and extra pens in baskets or containers so they are accessible but not visible. If there's electricity in the office closet, consider placing your printer and fax machine on a shelf out of sight, but accessible.

Grouping your office supplies in an assigned area will also help you keep track when you're running low on a particular item.

Setting Up a Filing System

Ineffective filing (or a complete lack thereof) is often the downfall of a home office. Yes, a good system requires some up-front work and ongoing maintenance, but it's worth the effort. My filing system is divided into two sections: Reference and Action.

- The **Reference** section includes the papers that are just that—simply for reference. This includes all paid bills, insurance policies, and any mortgage paperwork. These papers are the ones you know where to find if you need them, but they don't require any action on your part. They're purely for reference (referring to them as needed).

- The **Action** section includes all current and "alive" paperwork—all documents that require some form of attention, such as bills to be paid; an insurance paper that needs to be filled out, photocopied, and mailed; a dry cleaning receipt for clothing that hasn't been picked up yet; or greeting cards that need to be written and sent.

Problem — Solved!

When Hannah and Peter married, she moved into his small three-bedroom home. They used the master bedroom, the second bedroom functioned as an office for their business, and the third bedroom was set up for guests. When they decided to have a baby, they realized they'd need to either give up the guest room for a nursery or move the office out of the house to make a nursery in that room. After much consideration, they opted to finish off their detached garage and make it into a proper office since their business was expanding as quickly as their family.

Once they completed the renovation of the new office space, they began moving all the office equipment and files to the new space. They soon realized they had a horrible accumulation of unorganized paperwork that they needed to address in order to make the new space into what they really wanted: A place to meet with potential clients and perhaps eventually accommodate a couple of employees.

As they sorted through the paperwork, they came to the conclusion that much of what they had, both personal and business, were papers that simply needed a place to live because they didn't require any action. They sorted the papers by year, put them in labeled boxes, stored everything from the prior years, and then neatly filed the current year's paperwork in a filing cabinet in the office. Any paperwork they needed to act upon was sorted into categories and then addressed.

Although it was a huge undertaking, they managed to complete it, along with the nursery, prior to the baby's arrival. It was a huge relief for them to not only have a dedicated office space to work from, but that all the paperwork that had been a visual distraction was now gone, leaving a serene environment. Beyond that, they loved the nursery they created for their baby and actually managed to carve out more time to spend as a family now that the office was organized. In addition, the completely separate office space meant that they could actually close the door and "go home" at the end of the day, putting a stop to the never-ending workdays that they experienced in the past.

Setting Up an Action File

The Action system can be set up quite simply by using a portable container or using the drawer that is in your desk. Fill the Action file with hanging folders and label them with the following:

- Bills to be paid
- Discuss
- Mom
- Dad
- Calls to be made
- Letters to write
- Add other categories as they emerge. However, keep it simple—don't allow Reference items to live in this container.

Setting Up Reference Files

If you have a backlog of paper, follow these steps to organize it into a Reference file:

1. Sort paper into Bankers Boxes, using one box per year. Sorting by year is more effective than sorting by category because you generally only need to save the past year's documents (taxes, insurance coverage, and so on). You must keep your records that support an item of income or deductions on a tax return until the period of limitations for that return runs out. For more information, visit *www.irs.gov*.

Also, if you have an abundance of paperwork in your office, focus on the current paperwork first and store the older boxes (with documents from previous years); organize those when you have time. This way, you're organizing what is current and removing older stuff from the all-important filing cabinet. If you are current—meaning all paperwork from prior years has already been archived—sort papers on a tabletop by category. You won't need a Bankers Box because these items will be filed in your filing cabinet.

2. Once the paperwork is sorted by year (if necessary), begin with the most current paperwork and sort it by category (for example, paid utility bills, phone lists, insurance policies, and so on).

3. Make files for each category.

4. Put the sorted papers in the appropriate category files filed with the most current up front.

5. Place current category files in your in-room Reference filing cabinet.

6. Place prior years in labeled Bankers Boxes and store in an attic or closet.

Clearly label each box to easily identify what's contained and store the boxes in an out-of-the-way location. It's not necessary to have archived files within your immediate reach. Your files should remain active and current with only papers that you're currently accessing. All others should be stored and archived.

Where to Put Important Documents

❑ Centralize your most important documents in a fireproof container, which can be purchased at your local office supply store. This is the box you take with you in the event of a natural disaster. Having these important papers in a fireproof container can give you peace of mind, and may save the documents in the event of a disaster.

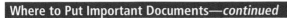

Where to Put Important Documents—*continued*

❑ Here's a list of what you need to have in a metal, preferably fire-proof, lockbox or portable container of some sort:

- **Personal items:** Passports, birth certificates, marriage certificates, diplomas, military papers, auto titles, insurance policies, mortgage information, paid loan records, appraisals of jewelry or art, photocopies of your driver's license and credit cards (front and back), and a master list of pin numbers and other log-ins (keep one copy in the lockbox and the originals offsite in a safe-deposit box).
- **Financial items:** Brokerage statements, stock and bond certificates, bank statements from the last twelve months, and other investment information not easily reproduced. Even though you may be able to access some recent bank statements online, consider saving paper versions as well. Some banks take statements and/or cancelled checks offline and charge you for copies later on.
- **Your Home Inventory list:** See page 231 for the form.
- **Other items:** Computer backups and other personal information not easily reproduced.

❑ Beyond your in-home lockbox, you should also consider renting a safe-deposit box at your local bank. Don't delay! If you don't have these items in one location, don't panic, but make it a priority to centralize and protect your records and documents. If nothing else, you'll have peace of mind that everything is safely stored in one place! Here's what you would put in it:

- **Originals to put in a safe-deposit box:** Birth certificate, marriage certificate, military papers, car titles, paid loan records, and appraisals.
- **Copies to keep in the safe-deposit box:** Driver's license, credit cards, insurance policies and cards, and passports.

Other Things to Consider

Now that you have your office organized, you should be sure you and your family are prepared and protected in a variety of other areas as well.

Financial Considerations

Now that you have a baby, if you haven't already done so, it's important to think about the following:

- Insurance—health, life, and disability
- College savings
- Will (including a living will)
- Retirement savings

Don't guess . . . get the facts and make informed decisions. Get referrals from friends or colleagues for a financial adviser. Don't just open the phone book and choose. Choose someone who will look at the big picture for your family and help create a long-term plan that will essentially put you on auto-pilot so you can focus on the fun versus worrying about what-if scenarios.

Also, try establishing a budget or a spending plan so you can accurately track your inflow and outflow of money and help identify if and when you are overspending. It's easy for new parents to overspend on baby—you think you need to have the latest and greatest baby items right away.

Making a Will

When a couple creates a will, it's also an opportunity to designate guardianship of your child in the event something happens to both parents. This is not an easy issue to address, but it's necessary. Talk to your spouse about guardianship.

Next, have a conversation with the person you're designating as a guardian. Choose someone who has similar values and goals in their life; someone who would love your child like you would and do what's best for them, including caring for their financial future.

Creating a will is a mature and responsible thing to do. If you die without a will, your entire estate—no matter how little or how big—winds up tied up in probate court and the judicial system determines who gets what. Your partner will have no say in the matter. One of the best gifts you can give to your family is to create a will. Consider all that you possess and designate an executor rather than having someone who doesn't personally know you and your family get involved.

Insurance

Finally, be sure you and your spouse are insured. There are numerous options for life insurance, such as term and whole life. It's best to discuss these options with your financial planner. You want to know your child is well taken care of in the event something happens to you. Addressing these issues will bring you peace of mind.

part two

organizing

for baby's
arrival

12 | Organizing the Suitcase for the Hospital

Congratulations—you're in the home stretch now! You're waking up in the middle of the night to go to the bathroom, unable to move at the speed you're accustomed to, and desperately wanting to wear nonmaternity clothing. Well, not too much longer. Now that your home is in order, we can talk about the fun stuff. Packing for the hospital is exciting! It means you're that much closer to meeting your baby face-to-face.

Problem—Solved!

When Julie began preparing for the hospital, she was a little scared. It was her first time spending the night in a hospital since the day she was born, almost twenty-eight years prior. Although she had attended various classes at the local hospital, including a tour of the maternity wing, she was still apprehensive about spending the night.

Fortunately, to her surprise, she saw on her tour that the birthing rooms were not as hospital-like as she expected. She kept reminding herself of that to ease her mind—she could envision where she would be. The rooms actually had a homey sort of feel, where the medical equipment was mostly concealed behind what looked like regular furniture. There were hardwood floors and upholstered chairs, plus a special chair for dad that reclined in case he wound up needing some rest during the labor.

A friend suggested that Julie bring comforts from home to make it feel less hospital-like. She brought her own pillow and pajamas, both of which really helped make her experience a little more personal.

What Mom Needs for the Hospital

❑ Your own pillow—It will make you feel more at home.*

❑ Socks—Your feet might get cold during labor and delivery. Your hospital may give you some, but bring your own just in case.

❑ One to two nightgowns/pajamas—You may want to wear the hospital gowns during labor and delivery, considering they'll probably get soiled. Save the ones you bring to wear after the baby is delivered.

❑ Robe and slippers—People will be taking pictures of you holding baby in the hospital, so wearing a nice-looking robe is a good idea.

❑ Underwear, including two to three nursing bras, if you plan to breastfeed

❑ Phone and address book

❑ Stationery/thank-you notes and stamps*—just in case you have time and you're feeling up to it.

❑ Blank birth announcements to fill in*—again, if you have time.

❑ Toiletries

❑ Lip balm

❑ Wallet, money, and credit cards

❑ Going home outfit—Remember, you'll want photos of this event. You don't need to look like a movie star, but you'll want to make sure you're comfortable in the outfit you're wearing.

* Nice, but not necessary.

Where to Put It

Mom's suitcase and purse

Leave your valuables at home. It's one less thing to worry about during your stay at the hospital. Besides, at this stage, you may not be able to wear jewelry due to bloating . . . or you may not be able to remove it for the same reason. Check to see if the nursing staff has a safe where you can place your wallet, money, and credit cards (make a list of what you're giving them). Otherwise, simply limit what you bring and put it in a safe place in your room or have your spouse/partner/coach hang onto it.

What Dad or Coach Needs

❏ CD or MP3 player (with music *Mom* wants to listen to!)

❏ Extra batteries

❏ Camera with film or card already loaded

❏ Video camera (make sure it's fully charged)

❏ Hard candy, lollipops, and other snacks

❏ Lip balm

❏ Stopwatch to record contractions

❏ Magazine or book

❏ Pen and notepad

❏ Back massager and massage oils for labor

❏ Call list or all relevant phone numbers and/or e-mail addresses in mom or dad's cell phone or e-mail account so you can easily send a group text or e-mail (with a photo, of course!)

Where to Put It

In a separate bag from Mom's suitcase. Let Dad pack his own bag!

Layette Items for the Baby

What's the layette? As defined in Chapter 2, a layette is the outfit and accessories baby needs for the first few days—for leaving the hospital and then at home. If you're waiting for the surprise of whether it's a boy or girl, choose a neutral color for the layette so you can wash everything before putting it next to baby's delicate skin. Use a laundry detergent made especially for baby to ensure baby doesn't develop a rash.

What You Need: Baby's Layette

❑ Layette outfit, including a hat (and outerwear depending on the weather).

❑ Diapers (eighteen to twenty). The hospital should provide them during your stay, but it's best to pack some, too, especially if you're planning to use cloth diapers (in that case, bring three diaper covers as well).

❑ Two receiving blankets—ask one of the nurses to teach you to swaddle your baby; there's usually a pro on staff.

❑ Formula and bottles—if you choose not to breastfeed. Sometimes the hospital will provide this during your stay, but again, better to be sure—especially if you plan to use a special kind of formula.

❑ Binky or pacifier—if you plan to introduce one.

❑ Diaper bag with supplies (see what to pack in the diaper bag on page 153).

❑ Carseat—You can't leave the hospital without one! Install the seat in the car a few weeks prior to your delivery date. If you're having trouble, generally the dealership where you've purchased your car or any retail store that sells carseats can help. In addition, many local fire or police departments have a trained officer on staff to check carseat installation. Call your local department for more information.

Where to Put It

In Mom's suitcase or separate baby bag—not the diaper bag, however (it'll probably be too full). The carseat goes in the car, of course.

Paperwork for the Hospital

As your due date gets closer, be sure you gather the important paperwork you'll need at the hospital. Put it in a labeled envelope or labeled file and pack in the diaper bag so it's handy. Make sure Dad knows where it is, too.

What You Need: Paperwork

- ❑ **Insurance card**—Including any information necessary to add a new member to your coverage!

- ❑ **FMLA/disability leave paperwork**—Speak with your human resources department in advance to ensure you have the correct paperwork and it is submitted on time.

- ❑ **Pre-registration forms for the hospital**—Your hospital may allow you to fill these out prior to arriving at the hospital, so when you do arrive, they have all the information they need and you can be admitted with ease.

- ❑ **Birthing plan**—If you have one. Not everyone opts to complete a birthing plan, but if there are specific issues you'd like the nurses and doctor to be aware of, such as whether or not you'll get an epidural and who will cut the baby's umbilical cord, it may be a good idea to write up a plan (see Birth Plan Considerations worksheet on page 214).

At the Hospital—How to Direct Traffic (the Visitors)

Once baby arrives, family and friends will be anxious to see her! They may even camp out in the waiting room. Discuss, in advance, with your husband/partner/coach how you want to handle hospital visitors. Remember that after you've had the baby, you'll be tired, perhaps emotional, and it's likely that you'll be physically uncomfortable. If you're breastfeeding, you'll be attempting to figure that out, too.

If you are the type of person who stresses out easily when there are many people around, you'll want to limit the activity in your hospital room after the baby arrives. Now—before you go into labor—is the time to begin establishing boundaries and communicate how you want to handle the time immediately after baby arrives. Here's a common scenario that unfolds if you don't address visitation beforehand and how to handle it.

Everyone Is Camped Out

Situation: Family members are in the waiting room while you're in labor. Baby arrives and everyone is anxious to get a peek at her.

Action: If Dad's up for it, he should thank everyone in the waiting room for coming, but tell them that after having the baby, you'll need to rest and would prefer that people visit after baby is home. If Dad is uncomfortable doing this, ask a nurse to convey the message. Then either Dad or the nurse can sneak in the people you really want to see. If the entire group insists on waiting despite your wishes, have either Dad or the nurse bring the baby to the nursery window to give them a peek.

Result: A calm and quiet recovery period at the hospital. Dad has effectively communicated to avoid potential stress and tension once baby arrives.

 good idea!

If you're looking for added quiet time once you get home, tell well-wishers that your doctor has recommended a rest period through your first week at home. Then Dad can limit the number of visitors to only those you feel comfortable with.

Introducing Siblings

If this happens to be your second child, consider buying your children a "big brother" or "big sister" gift to bring to the hospital when they come to visit their new sibling. This will help them feel important and not forgotten since most of the focus will be on the newborn. Also, assign special tasks to the older sibling, like retrieving a clean diaper, to let them know you'll need their help.

While at the Hospital, Have Someone Take Care of. . . .

To maintain your focus on baby, you will want to enlist the help of others on some particular tasks. Use the Delegating Responsibilities form on page 227 to help you. Assign the following responsibilities to a neighbor or friend:

- **Pets**—If you have a pet, ask someone to feed and/or walk it while you're at the hospital. Also, send a piece of clothing with the new baby's scent on it home from the hospital prior to bringing the baby home so the dog or cat recognizes the baby's scent. Consider enlisting the help of a dog walker to help you during the first few weeks. (See the section on introducing baby to your pet in Chapter 14, Organizing on the Go!)
- **Newspapers**—Have a neighbor pick up copies of newspapers on the day your baby is born as a memento. It will be fun to look back on the day's events.
- **Announcements**—If you have preordered announcements locally, ask someone to pick up the birth announcements from the printer or store.
- **Last-minute errands**—For the first few weeks after baby is born, enlist a neighbor or friend to pick up essentials when they go to the grocery store.

13 | Organizing the Homecoming

You have made it through pregnancy, the delivery, and the flurry of activities surrounding the arrival of baby at the hospital. Now it's time to bring baby home. So exciting! You have dreamed of this day for months. The carseat that sat in the house and the layette you carefully picked out are about to be used. However, keep in mind that this event can also be a bit nerve-racking if not planned effectively. Therefore, to head off the potential head-spinning, here are some strategies for bringing baby home with ease—who knows, he may sleep right through the whole transition!

What You Need at Home

- ❑ Quiet surroundings—But not *too* quiet, as baby needs to adjust to your normal noise level.
- ❑ Patience—Be gentle with yourself and those around you. If this is your first baby, especially, it's important to remember that having a newborn infant is a big adjustment.
- ❑ A friend or neighbor to stock your refrigerator
- ❑ A friend or neighbor on hand to run to the store for last-minute items

Problem — Solved!

Once the baby came home, Michelle and Jeff quickly realized that they'd be inundated with visitors. When Michelle's dad entered the house and said, "Let me have that baby!" because he was so happy to have a grandchild, Michelle almost leapt across the floor, wanting to ask if he had washed his hands, but realized that she may offend him by doing so. She quickly referred to a higher authority telling her dad that "the pediatrician" said everyone must wash their hands before holding the baby. He stopped in his tracks, and went to the sink without hesitation. Michelle's quick thinking turned into a regular routine when visitors came to see the baby. In the hall bathroom, she placed hand-washing liquid and some pretty disposable guest towels and a trash can. She told everyone, "The pediatrician said you need to wash your hands before holding the baby." And she'd shrug her shoulders and point them to the bathroom. Everyone wanted to hold the baby, so they washed their hands!

The Homecoming

Here are suggestions for an eventful, but stress-free, homecoming:

- Enlist the help of a family member or friend to take home the flowers and gifts received at the hospital. Remind the helper to empty the water in the vases before transporting to avoid spillage. Have them refill at your home. The only thing you want to be responsible for is you and baby.

- Keep the tone in the house quiet and the temperature comfortable. You will be recovering physically from the birth of your child and will probably be a bit sore and uncomfortable. Having a quiet home to walk into will give you and your partner an opportunity to peacefully introduce baby to her new surroundings.

- Have as few people as possible there to greet you. As much as people will want to visit as soon as you arrive home, have someone tell them you're not seeing visitors for at least a couple of days to give you time to get into a routine.

- If you want, arrange for someone to help you during the first few days. Enlist your mom, grandma, a sister, or a friend to spend the first few days helping you make the adjustment. Choose a person who is willing to do what you ask—or better yet, anticipate your needs—and not try and take control of the situation. This person can be there so you can have uninterrupted time to take a shower, eat a meal, or take a nap, especially if Dad is unable to take time off work. If it's someone who has baby experience, she can also show you how to burp the baby and other tricks of the trade.

- If you have pets, have someone else hold the baby while you greet your pet. They will have missed you and you'll want to avoid having them jump up and harm the baby (more on this later in this chapter).

 good idea!
Although it's tempting to wake a sleeping baby so you (or your guests) can "play" with him or her, you'll have plenty of time later on. New babies require lots of sleep and you need the rest, too.

What Will Likely Happen

Here are some common scenarios and ways to organize your response to those situations:

- **The baby will sleep through the homecoming**—Don't be upset, infants sleep a lot. Be glad he or she feels comfortable and is resting.

- **The phone will ring, a lot**—Let it go to voicemail! People are curious and will want to know how you are, what your birthing experience was like, and what they can do to help. Don't feel obligated to answer every call. You and your new family need to take time to rest and adjust. Better yet, record a message that says, "Thank you for calling, you've reached the home of [baby's name] who arrived on [date of birth]. She weighed in at [weight] and was born at [time]. Please leave your name and number and we will call you back soon."

- **People will knock on the door**—You don't need to let them in! Post a note above the doorbell that says, "Baby sleeping . . . please DO NOT ring the bell. We will call you when we're ready for visitors. Please leave us a note!" Put a pad of paper for the caller to leave a note.

- **Gifts and flowers will arrive**—Start a running list of what you've received. That way, no one will be forgotten when it's time to write thank-you notes. Keep the list handy and show your spouse and caregiver where it is to make sure every gift gets tracked.

- **Attach balloons or a sign to the front door**—Let your neighbors know the baby has arrived and minimize the number of calls and unexpected visitors during your first few days home by attaching a sign to your front door or attaching balloons in pink or blue to the mailbox. Have your neighbor who keeps asking you what she can do to help pick up the balloons and post them on the mailbox.

 good idea!
After a cesarean, your body needs time to heal—it can even be difficult to get in and out of bed. Therefore, have someone there to help you around the home for at least the first week or two. Get proper instructions on caring for your incision from your doctor. Most likely you will be given a prescription for pain medication. To be comfortable and get a good night's sleep, surround yourself with pillows. Most women say they started to feel better in a week to ten days.

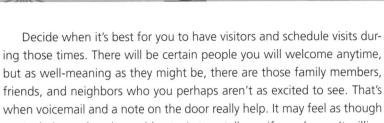

Decide when it's best for you to have visitors and schedule visits during those times. There will be certain people you will welcome anytime, but as well-meaning as they might be, there are those family members, friends, and neighbors who you perhaps aren't as excited to see. That's when voicemail and a note on the door really help. It may feel as though you're being rude or inconsiderate. Let me tell you, if people aren't willing to give you space and a chance to recover from the birth and establish a routine, I would be suspect of how much they are really concerned about you versus their need to catch a peek at the new baby. Those who really care about you will understand your need to get back on your feet.

Alert the Media—Announcing Your Baby's Arrival

In today's high-tech world there are many options for announcing your baby's birth, including the purchase of announcements from a print shop, ordering online, printing your own, e-mailing announcements, and mailing photo announcements. Some hospitals will even post a picture of your newborn on the hospital website for friends and family to view. Other services will mail the announcements for you if you provide the mail list. You can also enlist the services of websites where you can set up a personal web page to announce your baby's arrival, including a section for friends and family to make journal entries—it's a great way to communicate with friends and family worldwide. You can even try a webcam so baby can be viewed in real time!

According to Melissa Leonard, etiquette expert and owner of Establish Yourself, a New York–based etiquette consulting firm (*www.establish yourselfny.com*), some people are reluctant to send birth announcements because they feel like it might appear as if they're asking for gifts. But of course, it's not about that, and everyone loves to hear the good news of a baby's arrival. Melissa goes on to say that there is no set rule on how long after a birth an announcement needs to be sent out, but she recommends sending it within about six weeks of baby's birth.

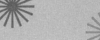

The birth announcement should reflect the parents' personalities. Choose the announcement style, the wording, and where you'll purchase it in advance. This is especially helpful if baby arrives early.

If you choose to not find out the gender of the baby and you want the announcement to say "boy" or "girl," perhaps choose two different announcement styles and wording. Then once baby arrives, you'll simply need to make a phone call or go online to finalize the order.

Problem—Solved!

When Miranda was pregnant with her first child, she was so excited that four months before she was due, she chose the announcement. She was far enough along to know baby was healthy and early enough to know that if baby did arrive early, she would be prepared. Since she opted not to find out the gender of the baby, she chose an announcement that suited either a boy or girl. She asked the printer to give her the envelopes in advance so she could address and stamp them. Miranda chose wording for the announcement that simply required the insertion of the name, birth weight, height, and date. The morning after baby Thomas arrived, her husband called the printer and by that afternoon, they had the announcements. Everyone laughed when they received the announcements just a few days after Thomas arrived. "How did she do that so quickly?" everyone asked. Okay—so she was a little excited about telling everyone her baby had arrived.

Recording Memories

You may have several different methods of remembering these precious early times in your baby's life. Here are some ideas.

Milestones

Use a calendar to record baby's milestones (birth weight, length, first smile, first tooth, and so on). The calendar will come in handy when you begin writing in the baby book or if you decide to make a scrapbook—you will have all the important information in one place. New babies do something new almost every day, so have the calendar handy the first few months.

Keep a Journal

During the first few months of your baby's life, you'll find that when the baby sleeps, you'll also probably want to catch a snooze. However, if you find that you have some quiet time and don't need to catch up on your ZZZs, write in a journal. Write down what you're feeling, or a special moment you and baby had, so one day you can give the journal to him or her as a gift of your thoughts. The journal will also be a great tool later on when your child is growing up. As children grow through different phases of their lives, being reminded of your thoughts and feelings about them and your hopes and dreams for them can help boost their self-esteem. Recording thoughtful and introspective moments or funny stories is a great way to process and internalize how you feel about your baby and will help keep track of milestones and experiences. Don't forget to leave some room for Dad to write, too!

Start a Blog

Create an online blog where you can make entries to update family and friends about baby's life—and add photos, of course! Blogs also give friends and family an opportunity to make comments and keep in touch. You'll also be able to track important milestones on the blog.

 good idea!
Consider joining Facebook—it's a great way to keep everyone informed about baby's progress without having to repeat the stories again and again.

Mementos to Keep

As soon as baby arrives, you'll begin collecting mementos to keep or to put in a scrapbook—everything from baby's hospital bracelet to the bassinet card. Purchase a keepsake box to fill with all the mementos, or simply use shoeboxes covered in pretty gift wrap paper. If you buy a large keepsake box, contain smaller items within it in a small, covered box.

What You Need

❑ The mementos you've decided to keep

❑ Containers for the items

Where to Put It

❑ Keepsake box—In the baby's nursery closet for easy access to place additional keepsakes

---

When organizing, it's important to decide how much space you are going to allow for a particular category. With baby mementos, it's easy to want to save *everything*. Begin by making space on baby's bookshelves or on shelving in the closet. Then designate a labeled box for small items, such as her baby bracelet from the hospital; another labeled box for all the greeting cards received; and a third labeled box for the newspapers, deflated balloons, and other larger memorabilia. Leave room to add additional items to each box. After baby turns one, add boxes for year two. Do the same each year. Keep in mind that you will be accumulating lots of memorabilia for years to come. Consider the space you have in your home and where you'll store the boxes. Take a proactive stance by choosing a box based on the storage space and only keep what will fit in the box during a year.

Choosing the Baby Book

Choosing a baby book is a very personal decision. Oftentimes, it's hard to know exactly what you want until after the baby arrives—especially if you have decided not to find out the gender of your baby.

There are many options on the market today. You can purchase a preprinted book where all you need to do is attach photographs and make journal entries. There's also the option to scrapbook all of your memories, where you create custom pages for every event and milestone. Whichever direction you choose to go, choose archival-quality, acid-free paper to ensure that it lasts more than your lifetime.

Keep it simple and stick with a book that requires little in the way of creative thought. You will have tons of pictures to put in albums, so strike a balance between time and quality. It can be tempting to get caught up in creating lavish baby books, but keep in mind—especially if you plan to have more than one child—that you may feel obligated to make such an extravagant book for future children, but you may not have the time. Think it through before embarking on the time and expense of a lavish book. Be sure this project fits into your soon-to-be busy life.

Photo Organization Tips

Regardless of which scrapbooking method you choose—if at all—you will need to keep your photos organized until the time you put them in a book.

Film Prints

If you continue to use a 35mm camera, consider having double prints made. Keep one set for your scrapbook, and put the others in an envelope so you can give copies to family and friends. (You'll save money by having the second set of prints done right away as opposed to spending the time and money returning later on.) If loved ones don't live nearby, pre-address and stamp a bunch of envelopes to baby's grandparents so you can easily pop a few pictures in the mail every couple of weeks.

14 | **Organizing on the Go!**

Don't women just love bags! No matter what the fashion trend, there's always a bag to match. Therefore, why wouldn't we want a diaper bag that's just as trendy and fun? In addition to choosing and packing the diaper bag, this chapter covers other on-the-go issues such as choosing a childcare provider, organizing your car, and traveling with baby (car and airline).

The All-Important Diaper Bag

All kinds of retailers now offer functional and stylish bags, but the key to making the most of the diaper bag is organization. First, though, let's talk about style!

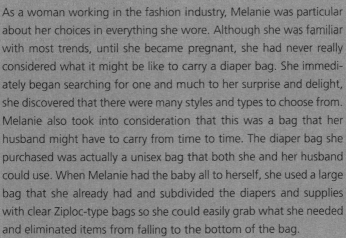

Problem — Solved!

As a woman working in the fashion industry, Melanie was particular about her choices in everything she wore. Although she was familiar with most trends, until she became pregnant, she had never really considered what it might be like to carry a diaper bag. She immediately began searching for one and much to her surprise and delight, she discovered that there were many styles and types to choose from. Melanie also took into consideration that this was a bag that her husband might have to carry from time to time. The diaper bag she purchased was actually a unisex bag that both she and her husband could use. When Melanie had the baby all to herself, she used a large bag that she already had and subdivided the diapers and supplies with clear Ziploc-type bags so she could easily grab what she needed and eliminated items from falling to the bottom of the bag.

Style

Maternity and baby fashions have caught up—no longer are pregnant women and dads of newborns expected to carry frilly pink or blue bags, immediately identifying them as a parent. You can find diaper bags in all sorts of styles—messenger, shoulder, backpack, and so on—and in all sorts of patterns, colors, and fabrics. Please see page 251 for a listing of resources for diaper bags. Here are a few popular websites for mom's diaper bags: OYikes.com, TristaBaby.com, and Ebags.com.

Dad Can Have a Say, Too

Don't forget Dad when you're choosing a diaper bag! What if Dad offers to take baby out for the afternoon so you can take a nap? You get baby ready and hand dad the diaper bag—but it's pink with cute bunnies. Dad's not going to be happy.

There are numerous inconspicuous diaper bags on the market today—even camouflage. Be prepared for the unexpected dad outings and consider choosing a bag that fits his style, too. If he wants his own gear, check out DadGear.com. This company makes a vest that has all the pockets needed to hold diapers, wipes, bottles, and a changing pad. It's a great idea for a hands-free outing. Or try OYikes! (*www.oyikes.com*), which also makes gender-neutral diaper bags.

Choosing the Bag

Choose a bag that has lots of pockets. If you absolutely have to have the designer bag with only one center pocket, purchase smaller zipper pouches for organizing items so they don't get lost in the bottom of the bag. Use several pouches to categorize what you put in the bag. For example, keep diapers and wipes in one pouch; bottle, bib, and formula in another; and a change of clothing in a third. Consider stashing an extra set of house/car keys in a zipper compartment in the bag, just in case you misplace your original set.

Baby Monitor

How you'll use it: This is especially handy if you have a two-story home. Not only will the baby monitor allow you to hear baby in the nursery while you're in your bedroom, it will also be helpful if you want to sit outside while baby is napping. You can even use the monitor to entertain your child by switching the receiver and speaker and talking into the speaker while baby listens in the nursery.

Where to put it: The main unit goes where baby is—most likely, in the nursery. The receiver can be placed in your kitchen, bedroom, or on the porch—wherever you are! Some sets come with multiple receivers, which can be very convenient.

Bouncy Seat

How you'll use it: This type of seat is a great place to put baby (generally up to 20 pounds) so he is semi-reclined. It often comes with a vibration feature to help soothe baby and an attachment with toys that baby can look at and eventually swat at.

Where to put it: Keep the bouncy seat accessible at home. It comes in handy when you need to cook dinner or fold laundry. It's also a small enough item to take with you to a friend's house or when you go on a road trip to Granny's.

Pack 'n Play (portable crib, or sometimes called a cosleeper)

How you'll use it: This piece of equipment is well worth the purchase, especially if you have a two-story house or travel a lot. Nowadays, many portable cribs come with a bassinet feature, so you can put the crib next to your bed and be within reaching distance of your baby until you want to move her into the nursery. You can also set up the portable crib for napping purposes. That way, if it's a beautiful day outside you can put baby down for a nap outdoors. Just remember to place netting over the top to keep bugs away from baby. This also works well at the beach.

Pack 'n Plays also work well as playpens, once baby begins to crawl and needs to be contained.

Where to put it: Master bedroom for a temporary sleep place for baby, family room for naps, or a great sleeper for baby when you travel.

good idea!

If possible, always buy items new to ensure the product is in full working condition. If you do choose to buy a carseat second-hand, consider buying from someone you know so you can be sure that it has never been in an accident, which could prevent it from keeping baby completely safe. If you choose to buy gently used equipment, check with the organizations listed below for any recalls or product safety information. Full contact information is in Appendix B.

- Consumer Product Safety Commission
- American Academy of Pediatrics
- Juvenile Products Manufacturers Association

Traveling with Baby

If you enjoy traveling, introduce it to your baby as soon as possible to get her accustomed to the sights and sounds of airports, train stations, and perhaps long car drives. It's all doable and can be quite fun. Here are some recommendations for organizing travel with baby.

Packing: General Organizing Tips

Much of what you will pack in a suitcase for baby will be a larger version of the diaper bag. However, to make sure you bring everything you need and want:

- **Allow yourself four or five days to pack**—you'll probably need this time to do laundry and prepare without missing something.

- **Set up a staging area**—Set aside some space in the guest room or a portion of your bedroom. Set out the suitcases and check off the items on your list as you add them to the piles. Make two separate lists: one for adults and one for baby. Check off each item as you place it in the staging area.

- **Use Ziploc baggies to organize individual categories of clothing for baby, labeling each bag**—For example, baby socks are tiny, so corralling them in a Ziploc keeps them together and you can easily see what's inside. Result: It's easier for you and others to find what you're searching for. You can also reuse the bags to put dirty or soiled clothing in them for the trip home.

Traveling isn't as complicated as it might all seem. The key is to relax, take a few toys, and just get out and be with your family. In the event you do forget something, it's not the end of the world. If you're staying at a resort, enlist the help of the concierge to get what you need. Or you can call an equipment rental company (see Appendix B for more information). The worst-case scenario is that you take a quick trip to a superstore and buy an extra.

Car Travel

If you're planning a long-distance family road trip, consider taking turns sitting in the backseat with baby. That way, if baby needs attention, instead of stopping the car or climbing over the front seats, one of you will be right there to take care of the request.

Assemble a car travel bag filled with snacks, books, and toys to entertain baby, a pillow for you, and possibly a blanket, lotion, gum/candy, and wipes. Remember to wear comfortable clothing. Remove your shoes and enjoy the ride.

What You Need and Where to Put It

❏ Music CDs—Up front and preloaded, if possible.

❏ Plenty of bottled water and snacks—If you're driving, place a cooler in the front seat (if a passenger isn't sitting there), or behind the passenger seat. Position the cooler so you can easily reach over and pull something out.

❏ Pillow and blanket for comfort—Back seat.

❏ Socks—Have a bag handy that has not only socks in it, but also lip balm and aspirin, in case you need it.

❏ Ziploc baggies for dirty diapers—In the diaper bag.

❏ Trash bag—Hang it around the headrest of the back seat and toss when you stop to fill up the gas tank.

Problem—Solved!

When Pam and John took their first road trip with baby, one would have thought they were traveling to a remote location where, if they forgot something, they would be unable to find it for miles. The back of the SUV was packed with everything they could possibly fit, including baskets of toys, DVDs, an exercise mat with hanging contraptions, a portable crib, portable high chair, a stroller, and more.

After spending most of the trip organizing the paraphernalia and later expressing their frustration to a friend, Pam and John were introduced to the idea of renting baby equipment while on vacation. Not only did this lighten their load and save them packing time, but it also simplified future road trips.

Airline Travel

Getting through an airport can be a huge production, especially with the security measures in place today. Make your airport experience a good one by limiting what you carry on. Use a baby carrier and a backpack to limit how much you need to carry with your hands. A stroller is great, especially if it has a place to store items below. You will, however, need to take baby out and send the stroller through security on its own.

Most airlines will allow you to travel with a child younger than two years old on your lap. If you purchase what is called a "lap" ticket for your child, here are a few suggestions to ease your trip:

- **Gate-check the carseat**—You want to do this so that in the event there's an empty seat, you can easily retrieve the carseat from the flight attendant and baby will have his own seat.
- **Wait to board the plane last**—Many times airlines will call handicapped and people with children first, but then you are confined to the airline seat until *everyone* else has boarded the plane. You especially want to wait if you've got a very active toddler and want to limit her time in the seat.

good idea!

When flying with an infant, try breast- or bottle-feeding upon takeoff and landing. This will help keep baby's ears from becoming clogged.

Equipment Rental

If you're visiting a resort or renting a condo, see if it's possible for the hotel to provide the equipment or have the concierge locate a company that rents baby equipment. There are numerous companies that will take your order over the phone, deliver the equipment, and pick it up when your vacation has ended.

Other companies, such as Baby's Away, offer rentals on everything from cribs and strollers to wagons, jogger strollers, and bath rings in more than fifty locations around the country. It's a service that has grown over the years because it makes traveling so much simpler for families with infants and young children. Check Appendix B for a few names of equipment rental companies around the country.

Weigh the costs—literally and figuratively—of arranging equipment rental at your vacation spot. Car travel and air travel differ in that you are definitely limited to what you can bring on a plane. If at all possible, add a carseat to your car rental. Today, most, if not all, of the major car rental companies offer carseats at a nominal fee.

If you're taking a vacation and staying in accommodations that have a kitchen, consider ordering your groceries in advance. There are numerous companies in vacation spots that provide this service. Check with the local chamber of commerce for a business in the area where you'll be staying.

 good idea!

When traveling with a baby who is already sitting up, especially to a beach location, bring a blow-up tub for baby. Bring it to the beach, blow it up, put it under an umbrella, and fill it with a little water so baby can splash around. You can also use it to bathe baby later on.

Choosing a Childcare Provider— Begin Your Search Now!

There are many childcare options to choose from today: in-home care with a nanny, childcare centers, family member, and in-home care at someone's home.

Before You Start

Be conscious about how you handle your everyday tasks. Analyze your routines and behaviors for a period of time. Make a list of the tasks and determine how you could make better use of your time when accomplishing those tasks. Rethink the way you handle your day-to-day tasks and challenge yourself to find an extra few hours in your week.

The main idea here is that once you get the dreaded chores out of the way, you can move on to having fun and enjoying your new baby!

A New Spin on Laundry

The laundry room can easily become a collection area for many things outside of its main function. The laundry routine can also be a challenge once baby arrives because now you not only have your own clothing, also but a slew of baby items—many of which are teeny tiny. Let's first talk about organizing the laundry room so it is functional, useful, and dedicated to its main purpose.

To clean out the laundry room of unrelated items that need another home, use the GOPACK method. The simple steps here are:

1. Remove everything from the room (minus the washing machine and dryer).
2. Group like items together.
3. Purge what's no longer needed.
4. Assign a home for the items that will live in the space (for example, laundry detergent, bleach, dryer sheets, fabric softener, spot remover, and drying rack). Consider a folding table if your machines are stacked. A table that attaches to the wall and folds down is a great way to go if you're pressed for space. Also, consider an ironing board cupboard and a retractable clothesline to hang washing.

5. Contain items. Do you need to install shelving or a cabinet to hold supplies? Consider containers (labeled baskets or clear containers) for socks missing their mate, loose change, and other items that are left in pockets.

Laundry Closet Organization

If you have a room dedicated to laundry, attempt to use the vertical space to gain floor space. Stack washer and dryer, if possible. Add a vertical cabinet with doors to house laundry supplies and possibly laundry baskets to conceal laundry in process. Keep floors clear so you can easily clean up by vacuuming and mopping. Clean the dryer vent regularly. Make the room a cheery place to spend time so washing and folding laundry don't feel like drudgery. Bring your iPod or MP3 player and portable speakers to listen to something that will make the time pass.

What You Need

❏ If your laundry room is essentially a closet, store only related laundry items here. See utility room organization (page 95) for storing other items.

Where to Put It

❏ **Shelving**—Place above the washer and dryer if they are positioned side-by-side to hold detergent and related supplies. If the machines are stacked, consider a closed cabinet next to the washer and dryer, so baby can't get into potentially hazardous chemicals.

❏ **Cabinet**—Consider a cabinet that can also hold a laundry basket so you have a place to house dirty laundry.

❏ **Retractable clothesline**—This extends the length of the closet where you can hang laundry to dry.

❑ **Sorter**—This will contain laundry to be washed and it's already sorted.

❑ **Bar**—To hang clothing. Don't forget hangers.

❑ **Ironing board cupboard**—Attach to a wall in an enclosed cabinet.

How a laundry room might be set up.

Organizing Your Laundry Routine

Start baby off on the right foot. Place a hamper in the baby's nursery for his dirty clothes, blankets, and sheets. Expect to do at least one load of laundry every other day for the first couple of months. Be sure to have on hand at least a week's worth of Onesies, burp cloths, and layette items so you can avoid doing laundry on a daily basis.

good idea!

For the first few months, consider washing baby's clothing separate from your own, using a baby-friendly detergent to ensure baby doesn't develop a rash. Although it's much easier to toss all of baby's clothes in with yours, using a baby-friendly detergent and warm water in a separate load will likely prevent baby from developing a rash. If, on the other hand, you need to consolidate your laundry loads for some reason, put baby's clothes with the delicate laundry and use a mild detergent for washing.

Start sorting! Laundry sorters serve a dual purpose. First, the laundry is sorted as it is placed in the basket, which saves time later on. Second, the sorter contains the laundry until it's time to wash it. A three-section sorter for whites, darks, and delicates works well—you could put it in the laundry room or the master bedroom, depending on space. Use a hamper in the baby's room since you'll probably be washing his clothes separately anyway. A sorter is also a great way to enlist the help of family members.

What You Need

❑ A schedule—Choose a day to do "adult" laundry. When baby is a newborn, as mentioned above, you will likely be washing his clothes more often, so if you can get your laundry routine in place it will give you a little break. If you do laundry on a specific day, you know you have other days off.

❑ Hampers and sorters

❑ Laundry detergent, for adults and baby

❑ Mesh bags—Place baby's tiny items (such as socks) in a bag so you don't have to dig through the washer to find these little items.

❑ Dry-cleaning bag

Where to Put It

- ❑ Post your schedule in the Family Communications Center.
- ❑ Corral the laundry—Place hampers in the nursery and bathroom, in optimum locations so clothes actually make it into the containers. Place in closet, bathroom, or near the dresser. Use a sorter in the master bedroom or laundry room.
- ❑ Place a dry-cleaning bag in your master closet since these items won't hit the laundry room.

Routine: Four Simple Steps

1. **Sort**—Use containers/hampers/sorters to make this step simple. Remember, if you're using a sorter, this step is already done!

2. **Wash/Dry**—Keep laundry contained until it's ready to go into the washer and dryer. That way, you'll avoid making a big production and have laundry scattered everywhere.

3. **Fold**—Leave laundry in the dryer until it's time to fold. Again, that way it's contained and not in a heap on the bed or sofa. If you do leave a load in the dryer, before removing laundry that's been sitting for more than a few hours, turn the dryer on for ten minutes or so to fluff it up, then fold.

4. **Put Away**—While folding, sort the laundry into like piles so putting laundry away goes quickly. Putting all socks together means they can be quickly placed in the sock drawer, all pajamas in another, and so on.

Avoid making a huge production when it comes time to do the laundry, unless you have a block of time and nothing else going on. Just keep in mind that with a new baby, there are likely to be interruptions and you don't want to wind up with a heap of laundry to be folded on the living room sofa. Try to take each load from wash to dresser drawers in one day.

Stain Removal

If you're not an expert on stain removal, you soon will be. Always have a stain removal spray bottle on hand, such as Shout. You'll most likely need to spray almost every piece of clothing before it goes into the wash, especially when baby begins to self-feed.

To avoid stains settling into the piece of clothing, wet the spot, squirt with stain remover, then wash. Repeat if necessary.

Consider posting a stain removal chart in your laundry room.

Cleaning

As mentioned in the introduction to this book, organizing and cleaning are two different functions. Cleaning becomes a chore when there's a combination of organizing and cleaning happening at the same time. Once you have used the GOPACK method, however, cleaning will become easier because there will be less clutter to move. You'll be able to focus just on the cleaning, which is the elimination of dirt, dust, and soil.

What You Need

❑ Supplies: Cleaners, paper towels, sponge, gloves, toilet brush, dust mop, and vacuum.

❑ Container to put all supplies in (bucket works well). Always contain cleaning supplies to avoid them getting knocked over and pushed to the back of the cabinet.

Where to Put It

❑ Utility closet

❑ Under the sink in the bathroom and kitchen (one set for each location to eliminate lugging of supplies from one locale to another)

How to Clean Up Without Stressing: Beat the Clock

Try these two tips before beginning:

- **Focus your tasks**—Avoid scattering your cleaning. Choose one area or one task at a time. Avoid attacking the whole house at one time because if there's an interruption, the house is left half-done. However, if you tackle the bathroom at one time, It probably won't take more than 30 minutes and it's done.
- **Establish priorities**—Identify what's most important and do that first. When less pressed for time, attack the least important tasks.

A Cleaning System That Works

Follow these ideas to ensure that cleaning becomes a regular, headache-free occurrence.

- Place cleaning supplies in containers around the house (preferably under every sink vanity in every bathroom). That way, the supplies are handy so you can take ten or fifteen minutes and accomplish a task.
- Regular "light" cleaning should generally include only dusting, vacuuming, scrubbing the toilets and bathtub, and washing down surfaces.
- Periodically (every three to six months or so), do a deep cleaning, where you wash the baseboards with a simple mix of cleaner and warm water and use a sponge to wipe down surfaces, clean light fixtures and windows, and change the air filters.

Attic/Basement

Be brave! Know what's in your attic and basement. Keep a master inventory list of what you store in the attic and basement spaces. Use the Attic/Basement Inventory form on page 210. The "date stored" column will help you see how long you've actually been holding on to the item and the "owner" column tells you who owns it. "Purpose" will help you categorize and clarify the item's meaning to you.

What You Need

- ❏ Containers
- ❏ Moth balls
- ❏ Cedar chips
- ❏ Labels
- ❏ Pallets to lift boxes and items off the floor in the basement in the event of flooding

Where to Put It

- ❏ **Attic**—If your attic is unfinished, consider installing plywood over the rafters to obtain areas to store items. Use moth balls and cedar chips to fend off bugs.
- ❏ **Basement**—Designate particular zones and label everything so you can easily locate what you're looking for when it comes time to retrieve the items you're storing.

✳ **good idea!**

When storing items in the attic or basement, use cedar chests or toss cedar chips into the containers. Reason: Moths don't like them. Your clothing and memorabilia will stand the test of time.

Label each box, and every time you put something in the abyss make sure you add it to the master list. Be choosy about what you store. Avoid putting items in the attic/basement because you're just not sure what to do with them. You're better off putting the items in the garage until you make a decision so at least they're not out of sight and out of mind.

Children's Toys

What You Need

- ❑ Storage in a closet or attic space
- ❑ Closed containers to fit toys, paper, and art projects
- ❑ Labels to label all containers with name and age range of what is contained in the box

Where to Put It

- ❑ **Nursery**—In the closet on the upper shelves. Keep current box you're adding to at a height you can easily reach to add new items.
- ❑ **Playroom**—In a storage closet or on a shelf where baby/children cannot reach, but you can access.

You are truly your child's biggest toy! They'll enjoy looking at you and exploring your face—without judgment, too. Get down on the floor with your baby or hold your baby close. Make faces and noises. They love it!

Housing Toys Elsewhere

Do encourage baby to play on her own, too. Have a central area for toys in the nursery and family room area, but also keep baskets filled with some toys in areas where you might need to have baby by your side, but occupied for a few minutes. (Much of this will happen when baby gets to about four or five months.)

For instance, if you have a home office and you need to get some work done, keep some toys in a covered basket so baby can help herself. Children enjoy the fact that there's a special place for their stuff and begin to look for it once they know it's there.

Designate a kitchen drawer or cabinet for things baby can play with. Toddlers will delight in removing and replacing plastic containers from a cabinet or drawer. Babies and toddlers love to empty and fill up containers over and over again.

Toy-Rotating and -Storing Systems

Rotate the baby's toys to maintain his interest. Set up a rotation by placing a large container with lid in a closet or the attic. Periodically empty the container into the play zone and refill it with toys baby hasn't used much recently. Baby will have fun getting familiar with what will feel like new toys. Rotating will also help you determine which toys were a hit and which were not, so when it comes time to purge—whether giving away or donating—you'll know which ones should go first.

If you're considering having another child, you may want to pack up toys and save them. Use large, lidded containers labeled with the appropriate age group (for example, 0–6 months, 6–9 months). Your child may enjoy playing with certain toys long after the age range of the toy expires, and that's okay—leave them out. If your containers are labeled properly, once your child tires of playing with a particular toy you can easily store it in the appropriate container.

Donating toys is a great way to purge and feel good about it because someone else will get to play with them. There are also consignment shops and eBay.com, where you can earn money to fund future purchases. Also, check out other online services, such as Zwaggle.com, where you can trade toys, equipment, and clothing for items you need.

Organize small toys in clear, shallow containers and label the containers. In addition to writing the name of the toy, add a picture of the toy on the container to help the child associate the letters with the picture.

Electronics

In this day and age, everyone's home is filled with all sorts of electronic devices. Though they usually enhance and simplify our lives, they also come with their own clutter and other organizational challenges. Here's how to tame all your gadgets.

What You Need

❏ **Inventory of what you've got**—Televisions, laptops, computers, camcorders, stereo, tuner, and so on, including model numbers, serials numbers, and the date purchased. Keep the receipts with this inventory and user manuals. Take it a step further and take photographs or video of each item, too. Store the list and pictures in a fireproof container along with other important papers.

Where to Put It

❏ Keep your user manuals near your electronics so you can easily refer to the manuals if you experience technical difficulties. You can put them in an expandable file holder and label each section appropriately (baby, kitchen, and so on). You may need a separate file for outdoor manuals and electronics since many people have lots of those items.

❏ Ideally, group as many electronics together as possible and keep the components in locked storage to prevent baby from interfering with them. Set up a station to make sure all video cameras, digital cameras, and cell phones are charged regularly. Purge outdated software and replace outdated components. Donate old computers, stereos, and VHS players to charities and not-for-profits. These organizations generally don't have much budgeted for new technology and are grateful for the donations. Back up your files regularly with a removable USB or a standalone hard drive.

Where to Put It—*continued*

❑ If possible, shift to wireless technology, which will eliminate many electrical cords. Laptops are wonderful space savers, too. They take up far less space and visually are less distracting. Another space-saving option is a flat-screen monitor.

❑ Consider an iPod or MP3 player that holds thousands of songs and load all your CDs onto one handheld device that you can take anywhere. Uploading all your CDs into one tiny device provides flexibility as to where and when you listen to your music.

❑ If you enjoy having your CD covers and liner notes, downsize the amount of space they take up by using a binder with sleeves that hold up to 120 or 240 CDs (fewer CDs if you include the booklet/liner notes). The storage binders take up minimal space and simplify the process of finding the CD you're looking for. It also makes transporting CDs much easier. You can use the same type of storage for DVDs.

Family Communications Center

The Family Communications Center (FCC) is your mission control, where everyone can see the family calendar of activities and events. It's also where you'll want to place paperwork (in a binder) such as phone lists, business cards collected, takeout menus, a running list of household projects, and baby items needed/wanted. Don't overload this section with old information. You want it active and current!

What You Need

- Bulletin board/chalkboard
- Calendar
- Pens/pencils
- Three to four envelopes or containers

Where to Put It

- Carve out a zone for a Family Communications Center on the inside of the pantry door or on a wall in the mudroom or laundry room. Maintain control of the family schedule and activities by including the following in your FCC area:

  - **Bulletin board**—Hang shopping lists, an invitations/activities envelope, phone numbers, hot lunch menu, and so on. Be choosy about what you add to the board and routinely purge what is no longer relevant.
  - **Calendar**—A two- or three-month calendar is a great way to see what's current and what's on the horizon.
  - **Pens/pencils**—Use colored pencils to indicate different categories (for example, purple for baby, green for work activities, red for social activities).
  - **Three to four envelopes or containers**—Label the envelopes "Invites," "Coupons," and "Bills to be Paid," and other related categories where you keep important active papers.

good idea!

If you're short on space, and/or have an especially mobile lifestyle, consider MomAgenda's All-in-one Folio, which has a seventeen-month calendar along with sections to hold phone lists, schedules, shopping lists, family medical information, babysitter information, and more. Visit *www.momagenda.com* for more information.

Compiling Important FCC Information

Establish a place in the FCC to place a three-ring binder that can house information you refer to on a regular basis. Here are possible sections:

- Phone lists—see page 179 for additional information on phone lists
- Business card holder sheets
- Running lists of the following:
  - **A list of baby items needed/wanted**—This will come in handy when someone asks you what they should buy for the baby.
  - **Household projects to complete**—Once baby arrives, many projects will go on the back burner. Keep a list and consider prioritizing it so when you do have time, you can simply choose a task.
- Takeout menus—After baby arrives, some days you may find it challenging to cook a meal because of the many interruptions like diaper changes and feedings—or because you're simply too darn tired! Add a section to the binder for takeout menus. Placing menus in the three-ring binder will be useful and helpful in those moments when you're asking yourself, "What am I going to make for dinner?"

You can easily customize your Family Communications Center.

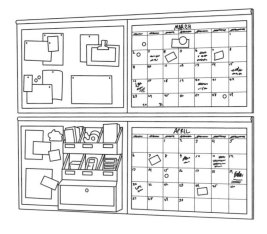

Phone Lists

Establish a master phone list on your computer (so you can easily change or update the information and reprint). Post the list next to the phone or on the inside cabinet door nearest to the phone. Posting the list will make it much easier to access with one hand; it will be even easier if it's visible. Of course, many of these numbers will already be programmed into your cell phone, but visitors or babysitters may need these numbers at some point. The phone list should include the following numbers:

- Grandparents
- Neighbors—reliable ones!
- Friends
- Family
- Pediatrician
- OB/GYN
- Hospital
- Poison Control—Don't panic! There may come a time when your toddler decides that tasting your eye makeup remover is a wise decision and you need to find out what to do. This is a fairly common occurrence that generally only happens once, because you quickly become hypersensitive after the first occurrence.

 good idea!
For backup purposes, you may want to place a second copy of your phone list in the three-ring binder mentioned earlier.

You decide, but again make sure you've determined how much space you will allow to house this category—and stick to it!

Grocery Shopping

Any successful event begins with precise preparation. For busy moms, grocery shopping can become a challenge. Before leaving for the grocery store, know the following:

- The budget
- What meals you plan to make (use the Meal Planner Form on page 244)
- How many people you will feed
- How many days you're buying for

What You Need

- ❑ Master list
- ❑ Meal Planner form (see page 244)
- ❑ Coupons
- ❑ Eco-friendly cloth bags
- ❑ Grocery cart cover for baby to sit in*
- ❑ A full stomach—Shopping on an empty stomach can result in added impulse purchases. Eat beforehand (feed baby too) so you can stick to your list.

* Nice, but not necessary.

Where to Put It

- ❑ Use one of the eco-friendly cloth bags to hold the other bags (folded), your master list, coupons, and a snack for yourself, if necessary. Place the bag in the car.

✱ good idea!

If you shop the outer perimeter of the grocery store, you're shopping healthier. Why? All of the fresh produce, meats, and dairy foods are in coolers along the outside walls while the processed and packaged foods are in the aisles. Supermarkets and grocery stores are set up to take advantage of the traditional pattern shopping consumers follow when they enter a store. It's most natural to go to the right when you enter, then go up and down the aisles. Try starting at the left and go around the outside first, then decide if you even need to go up and down the aisles and pick up other items. You may find that making one trip a month to a superstore may be the best solution for bulk items.

Online Grocery Shopping

Many grocery stores now offer online shopping. You log in, choose your items, choose a pickup time, and check out online. When it's time to pick up your groceries, you simply drive up and your groceries are brought to your car. There's no getting out of the car! Or, have them delivered to your door. Best of all, your shopping list is saved online and you can more easily avoid impulse purchases, saving you some money.

Labeling

Once you've established a permanent home for an item, apply a label to where it lives. Labeling is an effective way for you to quickly identify what you're looking at. It frees the mind from having to first identify what you're looking at and then give it a name. Labeling will also help others maintain systems more easily because they'll know where an item lives.

What You Need	
❑ Labelmaker	❑ Extra tape for the machine
❑ Extra batteries	

Where to Put It
❑ Utility room or kitchen

Designate a permanent home for the label maker so you can always find it!

Magazines

If you enjoy collecting ideas or articles, purchase a portable file container that holds hanging files or an accordion-style file container, labeled by category (for example, kitchen, bedroom, paint colors, and so on). Tear out the article and place it in the file, then recycle the magazine.

What You Need

- ❑ Container
- ❑ Master list of subscriptions
- ❑ File folder for saved articles

Where to Put It

❑ **Magazines**—in an upright container or proper magazine holders for those publications you intend on keeping for a period of time. Assign a limited amount of space so when the container becomes full, you'll know it's time to purge.

❑ **Master list**—in a file labeled "Subscriptions" in the Reference file.

System

- Place magazines chronologically in an upright container with the most current issues in the front; pull older ones from the back when the container is full. Put the container where you like to read.

- If you find an article or articles you want to keep, tear them out of the magazine, recycle the magazine, and file the article in your "Articles" file. Remember that 80 percent of what you file isn't accessed again. Think twice: Can you easily Google it? Do you want to manage that piece of paper?

- Share subscriptions with friends.

- Keep only three months' worth. To purge, simply grab the older publications from the back of the container and give them to a doctor's office, charity, or recycling. Remember to remove your address label from the publications prior to donating.

- If there are publications that you read regularly but find yourself buying in the checkout line at the grocery store, consider purchasing a subscription; you can generally save up to 50 percent on each issue.

Mail Center

Mail becomes an issue when there's no system in place for it. For example, if you have no "landing" place, it winds up in different places throughout the house, or you're not sure what to actually do with it. There are three choices when it comes to mail: File, act on it (including, but separate: bills to be paid), or toss. An easy toss: solicitations you're not in the market for.

What You Need
❏ Inboxes, with a specific "bills to be paid" container
❏ Trash can
❏ Envelopes, stamps, a pen, and note paper or stationery
Where to Put It
❏ Front hall or Family Communications Center

Avoid using a drawer or an out-of-sight container for storing mail.

System

So everyone's responsible for their own mail, designate an inbox for each member of the family (of course, you can monitor baby's). Open your mail with the trash can handy. Immediately toss any unsolicited direct mail offers, unless you've decided previously that it's something you've been searching for. Throw away the envelopes the mail arrives in and place the bills in a "bills to be paid" container to avoid misplacing them. Put anything to be filed directly into the Reference file cabinet in your office.

Recipes

Easy recipe organization can be done in three ways.

What You Need

1. Traditional recipe box on the counter.

2. Filing recipes in clear sheet protectors in a binder—this keeps the recipe clean and maintains organization so you can easily find what you're looking for.

3. Recipe software available online.

Remember that you can access many recipes online, so be particular about which recipes you choose to keep a hard copy of in your physical space. Of course, Mom's apple pie recipe that she originally wrote on an index card deserves a special place, in a special box in your kitchen! If you're using a recipe box or binder, label the sections as follows:

- Breakfast/Lunch
- Dinner/Appetizers
- Casseroles/Soups/Stews
- Desserts/Vegetable Dishes
- Snacks/Other (you choose!)

Where to Put It

❑ Place the loose recipe binder or the recipe box in the kitchen where it is handy—near the cookbooks. If you choose to keep your recipes on your computer, there are many electronic solutions on the market today. Do a Google search for "recipe software" to locate a vendor.

Six Strategies for Staying Organized

Here are six strategies for staying organized and keeping up the organizing systems you've just put in place:

1. **Accountability**—Ask for help when you need it if you're not sure you can hold yourself accountable to maintain an organized home. It's okay to ask for help. In fact, getting help will save you time, energy, and money in the long run! Contact NAPO (*www.napo.net*) to find a professional organizer in your area. That person can help make sure you implement the systems properly and then maintain them.

2. **Label, Label, Label**—Labeling will help you and your family members maintain the system you've worked so hard to put in place. If given instructions on how and where to place items, chances are that family members will rise to the occasion and maintain the systems.

3. **Honesty**—You've worked so hard to organize your space. To maintain your systems, make an agreement with yourself that if you decide to bring something new into your space, you'll remove something first. Make conscious decisions about the things you bring into your space. If you really don't think you need something, don't buy it.

4. **Donate and Consign**—Donating is recycling! Now that you've accomplished the task of getting organized, don't let clutter build up again. Make a commitment to yourself to "weed" constantly. Clutter is like weeds in your garden—it keeps popping up! "Donate" and "Consign" containers need to be a permanent fixture in your home, just like recycling containers are in most homes. You may collect enough items on a regular basis to hold a garage sale and earn money for the items. Drop off items you no longer need and commit to having those items picked up or dropped off on a regular basis (weekly or monthly). Many organizations collect used clothing and household items for people in need. Help them by donating and consigning your no-longer-needed stuff on a regular basis.

5. **Consistency**—You may be tempted to stray from the newly implemented systems. Don't! Remain consistent in your efforts to put items where they belong. If you find yourself slacking, return to strategies 1 through 4 as a reminder of how hard you've worked and the positive feelings you had when you followed through on your commitment.

6. **Simplify**—If you find that you haven't used an item after a period of six months to one year, be honest and decide whether you truly need it. Simplifying means reducing the steps to accomplishing the task; simplifying your life means to store things where you use them, eliminate unnecessary tasks, learn to say no, and covet your personal time. Make clear decisions about how you want to spend your time. Acknowledge that there are only so many hours in the day.

16 | **Babyproofing**

As I mentioned earlier, you don't need to babyproof the day you bring baby home from the hospital, but neither do you want to wait until he's already crawling. When baby sits up is a good time—he's making progress and will soon be mobile, but isn't yet.

Following is a list of general items your home will need. Also employ the tried-and-true method of crawling around on your hands and knees to see what he can get into—then lock it up! I've combined the What You Need and Where to Put It in a table format because some of the items you'll need go in more than one place.

What You Need and Where to Put It	
Item	Place
Smoke detectors	Every room
Fire extinguisher	Kitchen; if you live in a two-story house, have one on each level
Temperature guard on water heater	Where the water heater is located
Nonslip pads for under rugs	Throughout the home
Safety plugs for unused electrical outlets	Throughout the home
Cord stop for blinds and curtain cords	Throughout the home
Toilet locks	Bathrooms
Cabinet locks	Specifically in the lower cabinets in the kitchen; but install on any cabinets that contain non-baby-related items or baby-related items not for baby's direct use
Fireplace screen	Fireplace. Remember to place logs, matches, tools, and keys out of baby's reach

What You Need and Where to Put It	
Item	Place
Covers for bath spouts	Bathroom tub faucet where baby is bathed
Covers for stove and oven knobs that are located at the front of the unit	Kitchen/stove/oven
Doorknob covers	Throughout the home, to keep your toddler from opening doors
Baby gates	Throughout the home (see page 194 for more on gates)

Now on to specific, room-by-room babyproofing suggestions.

Nursery

Generally when you set up a crib for a newborn, the mattress will be at the highest position for the crib. Once baby reaches the point of pulling herself up and can sit up on her own (usually about five months), you'll need to lower the mattress and remove any mobiles or gyms that the baby could possibly pull down. Here are some other nursery babyproofing ideas:

- Move crib away from anything that could be used for climbing (chairs, bookshelves, and so on).
- Put a thick rug or carpet below the changing table for your comfort while standing at the changing table and in the event baby rolls off. (Remember to *always* buckle baby in while at the changing table.)
- Position the crib away from windows, heaters, lamps, wall decorations, and cords.
- Check all nursery furniture according to our safety suggestions with the U.S. Consumer Product Safety Commission (CPSC).
- Mount furniture to the walls so baby does not accidentally pull it over on herself (bookshelves, and so on).

Kitchen

Of course, you'll want to keep baby from having access to what's below the kitchen sink—typically, that's where most people keep cleaning supplies. Consider storing those items overhead. For instance, if one exists, use a cabinet over the kitchen sink so that hazardous and poisonous materials are way out of reach.

- If you don't want to install permanent babyproofing cabinet locks, use large rubber bands to hold cabinets closed. Eventually, your toddler might figure out how to remove the rubber bands, but you'll at least provide him with an activity and you with a temporary babyproofing solution. Remember to leave at least one cabinet or drawer for your toddler to play in.

- If you plan to hook a portable high chair to your kitchen table, be sure the table is sturdy and strong.

- Install a latch for the oven door and a stove guard to block access to burners.

- Install safety latches on the refrigerator and freezer doors once baby is able to pull up on them.

- Get in the habit of cooking on the back burners, turning pot handles toward the wall, and using caution when opening oven doors.

- Place all hot food and drinks away from the edges of tables and counters.

- Forgo placemats and tablecloths to avoid baby pulling on them.

Bathroom

- Make sure all medications have childproof tops, and that your medicine cabinet has a secure latch. Even better, store medications in closed containers and place them on an upper shelf in the linen closet.
- Place soft covers on the bath spout and knobs.
- Put nonslip mats in and beside the bathtub.
- Purchase a bathtub ring for baby to sit in (and never, *ever* leave baby alone in the tub—not even for a moment!).
- Install safety locks on toilets.
- Use a washcloth behind baby in a portable tub to keep him from sliding. Also, if you choose to bathe with baby, use a washcloth or hand towel in between you and baby so he doesn't slip.

Car

- Install an approved rear-facing carseat, always in the back seat.
- If the sun is strong in your area, put hanging shades on the back and side windows to block the sun's rays.

Garage

- Put all tools and toxic substances in locked or overhead storage.
- Make sure you have a functioning garage door safety sensor.

Backyard

- If you have a fenced-in backyard, make sure gates latch securely.
- Empty wading pools and store upright after every use.
- If you have an in-ground swimming pool, surround it by a locked fence at least 4 feet tall. For above-ground pools, be sure to block access to ladders or stairs leading to the pool.
- After it rains or snows, check for any collections of water in the yard and drain completely.

Baby Gates

If you live in a two-story house, put baby gates at the top and bottom of the stairs to keep baby from climbing up them unattended. It's great to give baby an opportunity to master the stairs, but you'll want to supervise that endeavor. In the meantime, keep baby safe from an unintended fall by using gates. You can also use gates to cordon off particular areas of the house. For example, if you have a combined kitchen/family room area and you want to keep baby confined, gate the doorways that lead to other areas of the house. Check out the Babyproofing section in Appendix B for companies that sell gates.

General Safety

Here are some tips that apply to the entire house:

- Consider clearing all surfaces at or below your waist.
- Install rubber stoppers that prevent doors from slamming shut to avoid pinching baby's fingers.
- Post emergency numbers next to every phone or pre-program numbers into your phones, including the number for Poison Control in the event baby ingests a potentially poisonous substance.
- Make sure you know whether your houseplants are harmful or not. If poisonous, remove from the house (one less worry about baby ingesting something harmful).
- Consider moving the pet's bowls to a closed-off area such as the laundry room. (Read more on this in Chapter 13, Organizing the Homecoming.)
- Have a first-aid kit on hand.
- Get any flaking or peeling paint sealed or removed by a professional, especially if your home was built before 1978 (dust from lead paint, which was banned from residential use in that year, can cause neurological damage if ingested).

- Cover all sharp furniture edges and corners with bumpers or safety padding.
- If possible, block all open outlets with furniture (use safety plugs when you can't).
- Always unplug and store electric appliances not in use (iron, hairdryer, flat iron, and so on)
- Always store your own and visitors' purses out of baby's reach.
- Secure heavy furniture such as bookcases and cabinets to walls to prevent accidental tipping.
- Put televisions and other heavy items on sturdy furniture, and move as close to the wall or corner as possible. Now that flat screen televisions are prevalent, hang on the wall or place up high and remember to conceal the cords.
- Move all tall, wobbly lamps behind furniture.
- Block access to all floor heaters and radiators. Toddlers may be tempted to drop small items into the floor grates.
- Use plexiglass to block any space of more than four inches between stair or balcony rail.
- Place colorful stickers on sliding doors and any other large panes of glass so it is apparent that there is glass, to keep baby from walking or running into it.
- Install window guards and stops, and put safety bars or netting on all windows, landings, and decks.
- Never leave any amount of water in an open container or bucket.

Source: Consumer Products Safety Commission

17 | Enjoying Baby's Firsts

Baby's Firsts

"Baby's firsts" are some of the most exciting moments of your first few years with baby. Who doesn't want each of these experiences to be memorable and to go off without a hitch? Each "first" comes with a list of details on how to organize and prepare for the unexpected—basically, what you wouldn't know if you haven't done it before.

There are so many firsts with a new baby. This chapter covers six of the most important ones and suggestions for organizing and implementing each one:

1. First bath
2 First checkup
3. First photo shoot
4 First swimming experience
5. First birthday party
6. First haircut

 good idea!

Set up an electronics station so you can easily recharge your digital camera and video camera. If necessary, keep extra batteries and film handy, too. You want to be ready at a moment's notice and not be saying to your spouse, "I thought *you* were going to recharge the camera!"

First Bath

Baby's first bath is an event, so treat it as such. With any successful event, it's all about preparation. However, as anxious as you'll be to get baby in some warm water, resist the urge until the umbilical cord has fallen off. Until then, give baby a sponge bath by simply using a washcloth with warm water, cleaning around her face, neck, and genital area.

What You Need

- ❑ Bathtub—Portable tub for infant, placed on a firm surface
- ❑ Washcloth
- ❑ Towel—Hooded towels work well
- ❑ Baby-friendly soap/shampoo
- ❑ Pitcher or cup to add water to bath or rinse baby
- ❑ Toys
- ❑ Camera and/or video camera

 good idea!

Remember that wet baby plus soap makes one slippery infant. Consider a bathtub that has a padded, slip-resistant seat and a buckle, if possible. There's also the option of using a baby tub with a bath sling that baby lays on, so he's propped up. Remember to always put the tub on a sturdy surface and never leave baby unattended.

Where to Bathe Baby

Because baby is so tiny, you can give her a bath in a variety of different places: in the bathtub, supported by a towel or portable bath; with Mom or Dad (again, remember to support baby with a washcloth or towels so baby doesn't slip out of your hands); or even the kitchen sink, supported by a towel or portable tub.

If you're using a portable bathtub, be sure it's on a stable surface—a kitchen table or counter works great because there's generally more room for Mom and Dad to move about than in the bathroom.

Tips for Bathtime

- You probably want to make sure both parents (or at least two people) are involved in the first bath, just in case you forget something so the other person can grab it. *Never* leave your baby unattended in the bath.

- Check the water temperature (the ideal temperature is 98 degrees Fahrenheit) and keep the water level low.

- To avoid startling baby when rinsing his head, hold a small washcloth over his forehead to keep water from running into his eyes.

- Remember to support baby's head and neck. Use dampened cotton balls to clean eyes, ears, and neck.

- Make sure you have a camera and/or video camera on hand to film the first experience.

 good idea!

To keep from straining your back and knees, use a kneepad that's made for gardening when bathing baby in a traditional tub.

Bathing with Baby

If you choose to get in the tub *with* your baby, be sure you have some help the first few times. Fill the tub about half or two-thirds deep, climb into the tub, and sit down. Then have dad or a helper hand you baby. Hold baby on your chest, making sure you are positioned so the water doesn't come up near the baby's mouth or face. Use a towel or a wash-cloth between you and baby initially, until you're used to holding baby in the water. This will keep baby from slipping out of your grasp. Have the helper stick around or return when you're ready to get out of the tub, so you can transfer the baby out safely, then step out yourself.

Once Baby Is Sitting Up

When baby can sit up on her own, you can begin to use a bath ring. These are fun because you can interact with baby without the worry of her toppling over. It also makes baby feel like a big kid if she can maintain a sitting position without Mom or Dad's help. Keep the water level no more than 2 to 3 inches and never leave baby unattended.

 good idea!

Use baby-friendly products to ensure baby doesn't develop a rash from products that contain harsh ingredients. You won't need much soap. Babies don't get really dirty until they begin eating solids and crawling. Unless you have a baby that is prone to spit up, a proper bath two to three times a week is sufficient (sponge bathe him otherwise).

Bath rings are large, but try to find a creative way to store it if you're using it in a shared bath and need to store it so others can use the tub. For example, consider hanging a hook for it up high in the bathroom, even inside the tub (at the end away from the faucet) so it's not under-foot and is available. Before hanging the hook, you'll need to consider how that placement would work when an adult is showering, of course (is the tub in the way if it's hanging in there?). You could also try attaching a hook to the wall above the faucet and hang it there.

 good idea!

Check out the Tummy Tub, a product popular in Europe that's now being sold in the United States. It mimics the experience baby had in utero because baby is in water up to her shoulders (i.e., covered much more than she would be in a regular baby tub) and in the same folded-up position thanks to the product's shape. Check out *www.bathedwithlove.com* for more photos and more information.

First Checkup

As soon as baby is delivered, the nurses will examine baby and record his statistics, including height, weight, and Apgar score—the measurement of a newborn's response to birth and life outside the womb. The Apgar ratings are based on the following factors: appearance (color), pulse, grimace (reflex), activity, and respiration. A high score is 10 and the low end is 1. This test will be performed twice: at one minute after birth and at five minutes after birth. Dr. Mary Ann LoFrumento, a newborn nursery pediatrician in Morristown, New Jersey, and the author of *Simply Parenting: Understanding Your Newborn & Infant*, says these scores have absolutely no bearing on the baby's future development. The test is done simply to indicate how the baby is responding outside the womb. Dr. LoFrumento further states that the only babies who get 10s on their Apgar scores are doctor's babies (it's a running joke among professionals in that field). Most babies receive 8s and 9s.

Oftentimes, the baby's pediatrician will visit the newborn in the hospital within the first twelve hours. However, the first formal pediatric visit generally occurs at the doctor's office within a week after bringing baby home from the hospital. Call the pediatrician's office when you arrive home from the hospital to make the first well checkup appointment.

In preparation for the appointment, write down a list of questions for the pediatrician—you will have questions, and it's best to write them down so you don't forget to ask while you have the doctor's attention. If you forget, however, you can always call later and talk with the doctor or nurse.

Keep track and bring a copy of baby's habits during the first few days. You'll want to track when you breastfeed and how often, diaper changes, bowel movements, sleeping, crying, and so on.

Tracking baby's habits during the first days will help you in two ways:

1. Establish a schedule.
2. Provide the doctor with valuable information to make recommendations where necessary.

The first checkup may be your first outing after bringing baby home. Get your diaper bag and carseat ready. Have your spouse accompany you or bring a friend. Have the following on hand for baby's first checkup:

1. Baby's schedule
2. Insurance card
3. List of questions for the doctor
4. Diaper bag

When you arrive at the doctor's office, you will probably need to fill out paperwork before seeing the doctor. Next, you'll be brought into the examining room where the checkup generally begins with the nurse weighing the baby and taking measurements to chart baby's growth. Bring a blanket for baby because you may need to fully undress baby for the exam. You want to keep him warm and comfortable when he's not being examined.

After the nurse has recorded baby's latest statistics, the doctor will then examine baby. This is your opportunity to ask specific questions and address any concerns you may have.

Prior to leaving, make your next appointment, which will generally be for a one-month checkup. You'll generally visit the pediatrician's office quite a bit during the first few years. The American Academy of Pediatrics recommends examinations at birth; 3–5 days old; 1, 2, 4, 6, 9, 12, 15, 18, 24, 30 months; and then 3 years, 4 years, and every year thereafter.

First Photo Shoot

Time to get a good quality picture of your baby!

Finding a Photographer

You may already have a photographer in mind, but if you don't, here are suggestions for choosing one:

- Ask friends for recommendations for reputable photographers whose style you like.
- Search the Internet for websites of local photographers. Visiting their sites allows you to preview their style and pricing packages. Ask the studio for references and meet the photographer in advance to be sure you like his or her personality. You want to be completely comfortable and feel like you can clearly communicate with the photographer.
- Do you have a preference of 35mm film versus digital? Color versus black and white? If so, be sure the photographer is equipped to handle it.
- Decide where you want to take the pictures. Do you prefer a studio or natural light? An artificial background or natural environment? Ask about location fees if you plan to go someplace other than the photographer's studio.
- Ask how they handle an uncooperative baby. This is important in the event baby becomes irritable and needs a break.
- Ask if he or she does mother-and-baby photos and family photos at the same time if you'd like to do that.
- Ask if the photographer can incorporate one of baby's favorite toys—either in the photo itself or to use as a distraction tool.

When to Schedule the Shoot

Karen Leach, a professional photographer in Los Angeles, California, says that it's important to get baby's portrait done as soon as possible. In fact, schedule sessions in advance to capture baby at one month, three months, six months, and one year. The key is to not miss the important shots and keep in mind that these photographs will become family heirlooms one day. Be sure you schedule the photo shoot just after baby's naptime or when baby is at her best.

The Day of the Shoot

Ask the photographer ahead of time if you can "shadow" him or her to get a record of baby's first photo shoot. This could be a fun way to record baby's first photo shoot experience or at least get one or two photos.

Another tip: Wait until you get to the studio or photo location before dressing baby in his photo-shoot clothing. Also, immediately put a bib on him until it's time to have the photo taken to avoid spitup and/or drool on his outfit.

Once the photo shoot begins, there is the possibility that baby will become uncooperative, for good reason. He may just need a short break to eat or a diaper change. Take a few minutes and relax, keeping in mind baby takes his cues from mom. Photographers who take baby pictures not only know that this can happen but anticipate it and build extra time into the shoot. According to Leach, a good photographer can get a great photo no matter how fussy the baby is. She says that she has never done a shoot where she didn't get something she and the parents liked. In the end, carefully choosing an experienced photographer can make all the difference.

Some babies will naturally be comfortable around unfamiliar faces while others will scream at the top of their lungs if they don't recognize the person. If your baby is stuck to you like glue, capturing a professional photograph can be challenging. Stay close by so baby is comfortable, but keep out of the shot.

To maintain your sanity and stable blood pressure, keep expectations low, be willing to go with the flow, and know that the experience you have with the first photo shoot is one that you want to make memorable no matter how frustrated you might get. If possible, consider bringing the other parent or a helper along. The extra pair of hands may come in handy.

good idea!
Bring one of baby's favorite toys for the photographer to hold near the camera to get baby's attention.

First Swimming Experience

Preparation will make this event fun! Start by adding a few simple items to the diaper bag: bathing suit, swim diapers (available at your local grocery or drug store), towel, change of clothes, a hat, and sunglasses—and don't forget the camera. Try a waterproof disposable camera.

For more fun, remember the Three Ss of Swimming:

1. **Sunblock**—If you live in a warmer climate, make sunblock application a part of your daily routine. According to Dr. Mary Ann LoFrumento, it's not necessary to put higher than 30 SPF sunblock on baby—however, it *is* important to apply it frequently. For maximum effectiveness, use waterproof sunscreen and apply it thirty minutes prior to going out in the sun. For a complete article on "The Truth about Sun Exposure and Kids" visit *www.staceycrew.com/pages/Resources.htmresources.*

2. **Swim diapers**—These diapers do not blow up like traditional disposable diapers do when submerged in water. Although they might be a little pricey, they're one of the best diaper options for taking your little one swimming. Do a Google search for "swim diapers" and you will also find cloth swim diapers that help prevent embarrassing accidents.

3. **Safety**—Never leave baby alone near the water. That should go without saying!

good idea!
Keep a beach bag packed with essentials in the car for unplanned visits to the local swimming pool or beach. Essentials include: bathing suits (for you and baby), towels, swim diapers, and sunblock.

Baby Turns One!

Baby's first birthday is oftentimes about Mom and Dad celebrating the milestone more than baby herself. It's an opportunity to celebrate with family and friends and perhaps a few of baby's new friends. It's fun to think that the baby really cares about the event. The truth is, though, that she's too young to understand why a bunch of people are standing around expecting her to blow out a fireball that's sitting on top of what appears to be some sort of fluffy pillow.

Themes, Location, and Food

If you want to use a theme, choose something that your baby shows interest in: A favorite toy or character will lead you in the right direction. However, you can also opt for a simple color scheme instead, accented by streamers or balloons. At age one, inviting a clown to the party could be a disaster. Remember, baby is little and adults are huge to them. Consider something more on baby's level.

An at-home party is an acceptable venue for a first birthday. Plan a barbecue or picnic for warmer weather or a buffet lunch and cake if you're housebound in the winter months. Limit the number of guests so that it isn't overwhelming for you or baby. Serve simple food. If you're expecting toddlers, consider a kid-friendly entrée and dessert.

Baby's First Haircut

When it's time for your baby's first haircut, ask for recommendations from other moms or check your phone book for kid-friendly salons, which are popping up all over. One of my favorites is a local salon that has what looks like amusement park ride cars where the children sit to have their haircut, which keeps them distracted from what's about to happen.

The timing for this event differs for every child. In fact, it may be that this doesn't occur for your baby until she is more than one year old. Either way, you'll want to make the experience memorable and not traumatic for your little one. Schedule the appointment when baby's at her best during the day. Prepare your child by talking about having her haircut, read books about baby's first haircut, and show pictures of you having your first haircut. You'll find that talking with your child in advance is great preparation because they'll know what to expect and be less alarmed by the experience.

Here's what you'll want to bring with you on the big day:

- Camera and/or video camera
- Baby's favorite toy or blanket for added security
- Plastic bag or container for a lock of hair to put in the baby book
- Perhaps a treat if that's what you promised your child in order to gain their cooperation

If Things Go South

If you find you need to abort the mission partway through, don't be discouraged. It can be a traumatic experience for a child to have someone cut his locks for the first time. Just reschedule and return another day. One day, the trauma of not getting through the first visit will be something you'll laugh about.

Appendix A

Worksheets

The forms in this chapter have either been referred to in previous chapters or have been included to help you organize various areas of your life with a baby. Here are the forms included:

Please visit *www.staceycrew.com* for downloadable versions of these forms, and more!

attic/basement inventory checklist

Oftentimes we store an item without knowing how long it's been in the attic/basement or what its actual purpose is, or we may be storing items for friends or relatives. This form is designed to help get clear on what lives in your attic, how long it has been in storage, what its purpose is (for example, keepsake or temporarily stored), and who it belongs to.

Date Stored	Item	Purpose	Owner

Date Stored	Item	Purpose	Owner

baby gear list

Log purchased or borrowed equipment on this list.

Date	Item	Owner	Condition	Warranty?	Price Paid

Date	Item	Owner	Condition	Warranty?	Price Paid

birth plan considerations

The Birth Plan Considerations form is designed for you to think about each part of labor and delivery. Keep in mind that you could be anticipating a long labor and wind up delivering more quickly than expected, or perhaps you are prepared for a vaginal birth but you have a cesarean delivery instead. Research and discuss the options online, with your doctor/nurse, and consult with friends who have already had babies. Various situations could play out. The objective of a birth plan is to make the considerations and be informed, but also remain flexible. Here are the areas to consider.

Labor: During the labor portion of the delivery, consider whether you want a minimal amount of activity in the room. Some nurses will not allow visitors, but you may want a good friend or family member there, in addition to your spouse. Talk with your doctor about who can and will be present, based on what you desire.

Labor Augmentation/Induction: At what stage will the labor be induced? Sometimes dilation doesn't occur in a timely manner. Discuss augmentation and induction procedures with your doctor and communicate your wishes to the doctor, keeping in mind your doctor has had experience with various scenarios. It may be best for her to make the ultimate recommendation; however, you can still discuss the potential options.

Anesthesia/Pain Management: Many women opt for an epidural. However, there are some who intend to have no painkillers. Discuss the options and, if you choose to have one, when would be the best time to have an epidural.

Cesarean: If you undergo a cesarean, you'll want to have your husband with you to hold your hand. As with a vaginal delivery, there are reasons why your doctor would consider a cesarean for you. This could be planned based on your condition or unplanned. Talk with your doctor.

Episiotomy: For a vaginal delivery, it's sometimes necessary to have an episiotomy. It's best to research and discuss how you'd like this handled.

Delivery: Who will be in the room with you? Do you want to be able to see the baby's head when it crowns? Do you want to hold the baby immediately after he is born? These are all questions to think about in advance. There's much activity going on in a delivery room. Each staff member has her own duties to perform. Communicate your wishes to the doctor and nurse prior to labor, if possible.

After Delivery: Who will cut the cord? If the baby must be taken to receive any sort of medical treatment, do you want your husband to accompany your baby at all times? I remember wondering if I would be able to remember what my baby looked like right after she was born. It was an odd feeling and I decided I wanted her with me or my husband at all times. This is common. Communicate with your husband about this issue and be sure you're comfortable if the baby is separated from you.

Breastfeeding: If you're planning to breastfeed, let the nurses know that the baby is not to be given a bottle (does this include not providing a bottle of glucose water?). Will you introduce a pacifier?

Photographs: Talk with the staff about taking pictures and video. Remember to take a picture of the doctor with baby and the nurses too.

Other: List any other personal considerations that come to mind that you want to communicate to the doctor and/or nursing staff.

choosing a childcare provider

Date

Referred by

Facility name

On the waiting list?

Date put on waiting list

Contact name

Address

Phone number

Website

Type of facility (for example, traditional daycare setting, church, synagogue, in-home care)

Caregiver-to-infant ratio

Experience of the caregivers

Staff training

Center policies

Cost per week

$

Vacation days

Facility closings

Summer options

Mom and Dad's notes

First impressions

Setting

Overall feeling

Names of caregivers at the facility

Overall

choosing an obstetrician

Choosing an obstetrician is a personal endeavor.
Use this form to record the information when you visit
the practice to effectively make your decision.

Date	
Referred by	
Doctor's name	
Practice name	
Address	
Phone number	
Website	
Office hours	
Hospital affiliation	
Insurance accepted	
Other insurance information	

Questions for the doctor:

Area of specialization

Call-in policy

After-hours procedure

Who is on call when you are not available?

Do you accept questions via e-mail?

Number of years in practice

Are you board certified? If yes, year certified?

Training and experience

When and where did you receive training?

Questions for the doctor (continued):

Why did you decide to become an ob-gyn?

What tests do you usually perform on a woman with my background (age, history, etc.)?

How often will I see you during my pregnancy and when do I schedule those appointments?

How will you handle medical emergencies during my pregnancy?

Do you or anyone in your practice specialize in high-risk pregnancies?
If needed, who is called in?

Do you offer childbirth classes through your office?
If not, who should I contact?

Will you be available to deliver my baby?
If not, who, what, where, and when?

Do you help me establish a birthing plan?

Financial matters:

Exactly what does my insurance cover for obstetrical care over the cost of the pregnancy? (Call your insurance company first, and then pose the same question to the OB office to ensure everyone is on the same page.)

What will be my out-of-pocket expenses?

What is your payment policy?

Other general information:

Your thoughts:

choosing a pediatrician

Doctor's name

Practice name

Address

Phone number

Website

Is the doctor board certified? If yes, year certified?

Hospital affiliation (including children's hospital)

Office hours? Weekend/evening hours?
How long is the wait for an appointment?

Call-in policy

Who is on call when my doctor is unavailable?

Does the practice partner with another practice when on-call?
If so, are these doctors board certified?

Are sick appointments available on same day?
Is there a separate waiting area for sick children?

Doctor's overall philosophy on:

Breastfeeding

Immunizations

Circumcision, if applicable

Sleep guidelines

Discipline

Using/overusing antibiotics

Vaccinations

Alternative medicine

Working parent(s)/single parent(s)

Other considerations:

Doctor's office location in relation to home/work/childcare facility?

Mom and Dad's notes after the visit (record overall impressions, feelings, and observations)

closet inventory

Get maximum use from your closet storage space. Begin by making a list of what currently resides in each closet, then determine if there's a better location. For example, if the vacuum is currently in the guest room closet, consider relocating it to the utility closet. Or if extra batteries are stuffed in the linen closet, move them to the utility closet. By addressing all closets at once, you'll have a clear picture of how to better categorize and reorganize your things.

Room	Before Relocating and Organizing	After Relocating and Organizing
Utility		
Master		

Room	Before Relocating and Organizing	After Relocating and Organizing
Guest		
Hall		
Linen		

delegating responsibilities

While you're in the hospital or at home for the first week, if possible, delegate household responsibilities. Add your specific needs to the list.

Task	Delegated to	Phone #	Notes
Grocery shopping			
Mail pickup			
Walk/feed the dog			
Water the plants			

Task	Delegated to	Phone #	Notes

gift tracker

Log gifts received and check off once a thank-you note has been sent.

Date Gift Received	Item	From	Date Note Sent

Date Gift Received	Item	From	Date Note Sent

home inventory

Perform a room-by-room inventory of items including furniture, electronics, and paintings/artwork. Identify the contents of each room, take photos or a video, record the serial and model numbers, manufacturers, and other key identifying marks. Store your completed inventory list and photos in a fireproof box or safe-deposit box.

Date Purchased	Item	Serial Number	Model Number	Warranty?	Price or $ Value

Date Purchased	Item	Serial Number	Model Number	Warranty?	Price or $ Value

keep it up tasks: daily

I (We) agree to keep up the systems I've (we've) put in place as a result of following the GOPACK method.

These are the DAILY tasks that need to be completed:

Task	Who
Make beds	
Put dirty clothing in hamper	
Put away toys and books	
Empty/load dishwasher	

Family member signatures:

_____

_____

_____

_____

keep it up tasks: weekly

I (We) agree to keep up the systems I've (we've) put in place as a result of following the GOPACK method.

These are the WEEKLY tasks that need to be completed:

Task	Who

(Examples include: Change bedding, wash towels, put out trash for pickup, and put out recycling for pickup.)

Family member signatures:

_____

_____

_____

_____

keep it up tasks: monthly

I (We) agree to keep up the systems I've (we've) put in place as a result of following the GOPACK method.

These are the MONTHLY tasks that need to be completed:

Task	Who

(Examples include: Drop off items for donation, clean baseboards, change air filters, file paid bills and other paperwork, backup computer, and shred documents.)

Family member signatures:

_____

_____

_____

_____

keep it up tasks: semiannual

I (We) agree to keep up the systems I've (we've) put in place as a result of following the GOPACK method.

These are the SEMIANNUAL tasks that need to be completed:

Task	Who

(Examples include: Change batteries in smoke detectors, inspect gutters and downspouts for clogs, and hire a professional to flush the air conditioning unit's primary drain line; rotate children's toys to keep space uncluttered and renewed interest in playthings; and change over seasonal wardrobe and edit clothing for donation/consignment.)

Family member signatures:

_____

_____

_____

_____

keep it up tasks: annual

I (We) agree to keep up the systems I've (we've) put in place as a result of following the GOPACK method.

These are the ANNUAL tasks that need to be completed:

Task	Who

(Examples include: Organize garage, powerwash house, clean carpets to remove deep-down dirt, and declutter closets, including linen closet.)

Family member signatures:

_____

_____

_____

_____

map form

Date	
Space	
Goal	
Zones	

TASK	Date Scheduled	Date Completed
Group **O**bjects		
Choose a charity for the Purge stage		
Purge		
Call to have items picked up, or drop off items yourself		
Collect tax receipt		
Assign a home for items		
Purchase containers, if necessary		
Qty. Size Description		
Containerize		
Keep It Up		

Reward	

map form

Date	
Space	
Goal	
Zones	

TASK	Date Scheduled	Date Completed
Group **O**bjects		
Choose a charity for the Purge stage		
Purge		
Call to have items picked up, or drop off items yourself		
Collect tax receipt		
Assign a home for items		
Purchase containers, if necessary		
Qty. Size Description		
Containerize		
Keep It Up		

Reward	

map form

Date	
Space	
Goal	
Zones	

TASK	Date Scheduled	Date Completed
Group **O**bjects		
Choose a charity for the Purge stage		
Purge		
Call to have items picked up, or drop off items yourself		
Collect tax receipt		
Assign a home for items		
Purchase containers, if necessary Qty.　　Size　　　Description		
Containerize		
Keep It Up		

Reward	

map form

Date	
Space	
Goal	
Zones	

TASK	Date Scheduled	Date Completed
Group **O**bjects		
Choose a charity for the Purge stage		
Purge		
Call to have items picked up, or drop off items yourself		
Collect tax receipt		
Assign a home for items		
Purchase containers, if necessary		
Qty. Size Description		
Containerize		
Keep It Up		

Reward	

map form

Date	
Space	
Goal	
Zones	

TASK	Date Scheduled	Date Completed
Group **O**bjects		
Choose a charity for the Purge stage		
Purge		
Call to have items picked up, or drop off items yourself		
Collect tax receipt		
Assign a home for items		
Purchase containers, if necessary Qty. Size Description		
Containerize		
Keep It Up		

Reward	

meal planner

No more last-minute meals. Plan out what you'll eat for the week, everything from breakfast to dinner, including snacks. Then transfer the items to a grocery list by category, which will make getting in and out of the grocery store quick and easy. Better yet, consider shopping online. Use the forms on the following pages to help you.

Meal	Sunday	Monday	Tuesday	Wednesday	Thursday	Friday	Saturday
Breakfast							
Snack							
Lunch							
Snack							
Dinner							

Meal	Sunday	Monday	Tuesday	Wednesday	Thursday	Friday	Saturday
Breakfast							
Snack							
Lunch							
Snack							
Dinner							

Meal	Sunday	Monday	Tuesday	Wednesday	Thursday	Friday	Saturday
Breakfast							
Snack							
Lunch							
Snack							
Dinner							

Meal	Sunday	Monday	Tuesday	Wednesday	Thursday	Friday	Saturday
Breakfast							
Snack							
Lunch							
Snack							
Dinner							

Resources

Baby Announcements

www.ofoto.com

www.photoworks.com

www.sendomatic.com

www.shutterfly.com

www.smugmug.com

www.snapfish.com

www.tinyprints.com

Baby Equipment Rental

Baby's Away
www.babysaway.com

www.thenewparentsguide.com/
baby-equipment-rentals.htm

The New Parents Guide lists resources for all fifty United States and more than half a dozen companies outside the United States.

Babyproofing

Babies R Us
www.babiesrus.com

Kid Safe Inc.
www.kidsafeinc.com

One Step Ahead
www.onestepahead.com

Right Start
www.rightstart.com

Safe Start Baby
www.safestartbaby.com

Babysitter Services

Sittercity.com
www.sittercity.com

Babysitters4hire
www.babysitters4hire.com

Bedding

Babies R Us
www.babiesrus.com

BabyAge.com
www.babyage.com

Carousel Designs
www.babybedding.com/

The Company Store
www.companystore.com

Land of Nod
www.landofnod.com

Pottery Barn Kids
www.potterybarnkids.com

Target
www.target.com

Breastfeeding

LA LECHE LEAGUE INTERNATIONAL

(800) LALECHE

www.lalecheleague.org

THE NATIONAL WOMEN'S HEALTH INFORMATION CENTER

www.4woman.gov

A project of the U.S. Department of Health and Human Services Office of Women's Health.

Car Accessories

Case Logic
www.caselogic.com

Child Safety

THE AMERICAN ASSOCIATION OF POISON CONTROL CENTERS

www.aapc.org

Find the Poison Control Center nearest to you.

AUTOMOTIVE SAFETY PROGRAM

www.preventinjury.org/specneeds.asp

National leader and expert in the transportation of children with special health care needs.

CONSUMER SAFETY PRODUCT COMMISSION

www.cpsc.gov

(800) 638-2772

For safety recall information.

THE INTERNATIONAL ASSOCIATION FOR CHILD SAFETY

www.iafcs.org

(888) 677-IACS

Child Safety—cont.

THE NATIONAL HIGHWAY TRAFFIC SAFETY ADMINISTRATION

www.nhtsa.dot.gov

(888) DASH2DOT

Information on child passenger safety and carseat inspections.

NATIONAL SAFE KIDS CAMPAIGN

www.safekids.org

(800) 441-1888

SAFETY BELT SAFE USA

www.carseat.org

(800) 745-SAFE

National, nonprofit organization dedicated to child passenger safety.

Closet Organization

Are You Organized?
www.areyouorganized.com

California Closets
www.calclosets.com

ClosetMaid
www.closetmaid.com

EasyClosets.com
www.easyclosets.com

Cribs and Furniture

Babies R Us
www.babiesrus.com

Ikea
www.ikea.com

JC Penney
www.jcpenney.com

Oeuf
www.oeufnyc.com

Target
www.target.com

Containers and Storage

Container Store
www.containerstore.com

Get Squared Away
www.getsquaredaway.com

Hold Everything
www.holdeverything.com

Ikea
www.ikea.com

Levenger
www.levenger.com

Lillian Vernon
www.lillianvernon.com

Organization, Etc.
www.org-etc.com

Organize.com
www.organize.com

Containers and Storage—cont.

Organize Everything
www.organize-everything.com

Organize Your World
www.organizeyourworld.com

The Organized Parent
www.theorganizedparent.com

Pottery Barn
www.potterybarn.com

Rubbermaid
www.rubbermaid.com

Spacesaver
www.spacesaver.com

Stacks and Stacks
www.stacksandstacks.com

Shelf Cover
www.shelfcover.com

Target
www.target.com

Diaper Bags

All Modern Baby
www.allmodernbaby.com

Babies "R" Us
www.babiesrus.com

Dad Gear
www.dadgear.com

Diaper Bags.com
www.diaperbags.com

Diaper Bags—cont.

Diaper Dude
www.diaperdude.com

Ebags
www.ebags.com

Giggle
www.giggle.com

JC Penney
www.jcpenney.com

Modern Day Dad
astore.amazon.com/moderndaydad-20

Oyikes
www.oyikes.com
For unisex bags.

Pottery Barn Kids
www.potterybarnkids.com

Skiphop
www.skiphop.com

Trista Baby
www.tristababy.com

Donating

Big Brothers and Big Sisters
www.bbbsa.org

Good Will Industries
www.goodwill.org

Junior League International
www.ajli.org

Especially for Fathers

ASK MR. DAD

www.mrdad.com

Armin Brott, noted author on fathering, has some down-to-earth advice for today's dads.

THE NATIONAL CENTER FOR FATHERING

www.fathers.com

Offers support and education for fathers and fathers-to-be.

PICKLES AND ICE CREAM

www.picklesandicecream.info

Great resource for expectant fathers written by an experienced obstetrician.

Especially for Mothers

BABY PLANNING

www2.itsa-belly.com

Itsabelly Baby Concierge Service, helping moms-to-be navigate the planning for baby.

DEPRESSION AFTER DELIVERY

www.depressionafterdelivery.com

Nonprofit organization providing support for women with antepartum or post-partum disorders.

(800) 944-4PPD (4773)

Especially for Mothers—cont.

MOTHERS AND MORE

www.mothersandmore.org

Nonprofit organization dedicated to improving the lives of mothers through support, education, and advocacy.

POSTPARTUM SUPPORT INTERNATIONAL

www.postpartum.net

(805) 967-7636

Etiquette

www.establishyourselfny.com
Melissa Leonard, Establish Yourself, teaches etiquette to children and adults in a corporate setting.

Miss Manners (Judith Martin)
Look for her books on Amazon.com.

The Emily Post Institute
www.emilypost.com

Garage Organization

The Art of Storage
www.theartofstorage.com

Garagetek
www.garagetek.com

Home Depot
www.homedepot.com

Lowes
www.lowes.com

Sears
www.sears.com

General Parenting Information

THE AMERICAN ACADEMY OF PEDIATRICS

www.aap.org

The official website for the AAP, offering advice and information on a multitude of pediatric topics.

THE AMERICAN SOCIAL HEALTH ASSOCIATION

www.vaccines.ashastd.org

THE CENTERS FOR DISEASE CONTROL

www.cdc.gov

WWW.IVILLAGE.COM

Dedicated exclusively to connecting women through all stages of life.

KIDSHEALTH

www.kidshealth.org

The official site for the Nemours Foundation, a nonprofit organization dedicated to children's health.

THE NATIONAL PARENTING CENTER

www.tnpc.com

Reviews of products and services for children and their parents.

General Parenting Information—cont.

THE RED CROSS

www.redcross.org

For information on First Aid and CPR training.

THE SUDDEN INFANT DEATH SYNDROME (SIDS) ALLIANCE

www.sidsalliance.org

Information on sudden infant death, the Back to Sleep program, and safe sleep practices.

THE BACK TO SLEEP PROGRAM

www.nichd.nih.gov/sids/

For information on safe sleep practices.

Maternity Clothing

Blossom Maternity
www.blossommaternity.com

Gap
www.*gap.com*

JC Penney
www.*jcpenney.com*

Kohl's
www.kohls.com

Mimi Maternity
www.mimimaternity.com

Motherhood Maternity
www.motherhoodmaternity.com

Maternity Clothing—cont.

Old Navy
www.oldnavy.com

Pea in the Pod
www.peainthepod.com

Sears
www.sears.com

Meal Planning

The Frantic Woman's Guide to Feeding
Family & Friends
www.maryjorulnick.com/books.html

Dinner A Fare
www.dinnerafare.com

Dream Dinners
www.dreamdinners.com

The Six O'Clock Scramble
www.sixoclockscramble.com

Office Products

Hold Everything
www.holdeverything.com

Humanscale
www.humanscale.com

Levenger
www.levenger.com

MomAgenda
www.momagenda.com

Office Depot
www.officedepot.com

Office Products—cont.

Office Max
www.officemax.com

Organize.com
www.organize.com

See Jane Work
www.seejanework.com

Staples
www.staples.com

Ultimate Office
www.ultimateoffice.com

Sharing Service

Zwaggle.com
www.zwaggle.com

Transitional Clothing

Belly Basics
www.bellybasics.com

Majamas
www.majamas.com

Motherhood Maternity
www.motherhood.com

Target
www.target.com

Tummy Style.com
www.tummystyle.com

index

About the Author

STACEY L. CREW is a mom, organizing expert, author, and speaker with a personal and professional organizing company currently based in Charleston, South Carolina.

A New Jersey native, Stacey has a high-tech marketing and publishing background. After working for many years with individuals who struggled with disorganization, Stacey's strengths led her to create systems to raise her level of efficiency in inefficient environments. Her experience has led her to develop a system that everyone can use to get organized—the GOPACK method.

Stacey has always been organized, but after moving three times in four years, she discovered decluttering and the benefits of lightening her load. She extensively re-evaluated what's most important in her life and began to declutter emotionally and physically. Although her professional life remains busy, she is more productive and has room in her schedule to focus quality time and energy on her two daughters.